Robin 'Hood 2000

A Pantomime adventure
of
Fancy, Farce and Frivolity

by

Michael Buchanan-Smart

Jasper Publishing
I Broad St Hemel Hempstead Herts HP2 5BW
Tel; 01442 63461 Fax; 01442 217102

To obtain information about acting fees payable on all professional and amateur performances of this play, together with any other details, please apply to the publishers;

Jasper Publishing

1 Broad Street Hemel Hempstead
Herts HP2 5BW
Tel; 01442 63461 Fax; 01442 217102

A licence application must be made before any rehearsals commence, and fees are payable in advance.

ISBN 1 874009 81 3

CHARACTERS

ROBIN HOOD	*(Sir Robin of Loxsly - Principal Boy)*
MAID MARION	*(Royal Ward - Principal Girl)*
DISHY DOLLY BROWN	*(Maid Marion's Maid - Dame)*
FRIAR TUCK-IN	*(A Holy Man)*
WILL SCARLETT	*(Robin's Nephew)*
MYSTIC MOG	*(Fortune-Teller)*
PRINCE JOHN	*(King Richard's brother)*
SHERIFF OF NOTTINGHAM	*(The Bogey Man)*
PING and **PONG**	*(The Sheriff's Men)*
MUNCH	*(Miller's Son - a Scout)*
FRED	*(Dancing Bear)*

Other named roles

KING RICHARD I	*(Richard the Lionheart)*
LOTTERY	*(King Richard's Messenger)*
LITTLE JOHN	*(Big Man)*
STINKER	*(Tinker)*
FEARLESS FIONA	*(Friend of Marion)*
HERA	*(Lady Protector of the Forest)*
LUCY LOCKIT	*(Dungeon Mistress)*
SIR GUY OF GISBORNE	*(The Black Knight)*
JULIE	*(Tinker's Daughter - a Guide)*
ROB and **BOB**	*(Village Lads)*
ANNA and **EMMA**	*(Dolly's 'children')*
SNIFFER	*(Tinker's dog)*
TASTY	*(Goose)*
PENNY	*(Penguin)*
PERCY	*(Penny's Brother)*
TWIT	*(Owl)*

CHORUS AS APPROPRIATE: MERRY MAIDS & MEN, SOLDIERS, YOUNG DEER, CUBS/BROWNIES, FOREST ANIMALS ETC., DOUBLING UP IS POSSIBLE.

Note; there is little mention of children/ladies in the tales - I have introduced some new characters to cater for this aspect

GENERAL NOTE; ROBIN HOOD is an 'Adventure'. It has quite a large cast but instead of having a chorus as is normal practice, most players have been given names. They should feel more involved as they are now actual characters in the pantomime.

SYNOPSIS OF SCENES

PROLOGUE

ACT 1

SCENE 1	SHERWOOD VILLAGE - MAY DAY
SCENE 1a	TALKING ANIMALS
SCENE 2	FOREST HIGHWAY
SCENE 2a	A SMELLY AFFAIR
SCENE 3	SHERWOOD FOREST - THE ROYAL OAK

ACT 2

SCENE 1	NOTTINGHAM CASTLE - TOURNAMENT
SCENE 2	DAME'S DELIGHT
SCENE 3	NOTTINGHAM CASTLE - THE RESCUE
SCENE 4	SINGALONG then NOBLE WEDDING

All scenes may be played with backcloths and side tabs, or; set for tournament/ Castle grounds, if appropriate

Overall, the Pantomime has been structured to minimize costs on both scenery and costumes

SCENES CAN BE AS SIMPLE OR AS LAVISH AS YOU WISH. FOR IMPACT USE RICH GREENS AND BROWNS IN ACT 1, SCENE 3, AND GOLD/RED COLOURS SHOULD ABOUND IN ACT 2, SCENE 1.

PLEASE NOTE: Primarily, the new 'Drury Lane' standards are used within the text: PS = PROMPT SIDE; OPS = OPPOSITE PROMPT SIDE

OTHER PANTOMIMES by MICHAEL BUCHANAN-SMART

OVER THE MOON *(Hey Diddle Diddle)*
SPELLBOUND *(Fairies and Witches in Sleeping Beauty)*
RAPUNZEL *(Let Down Your Hair)*

DESCRIPTION OF CHARACTERS

ROBIN HOOD. Dashing and brave as portrayed in the legends. Takes everything in his stride, and laughs in the face of conflict. A duty bound loyalist to King Richard. A forthright Hero. *(Female, juvenile or twenties)*

MAID MARION. Very delicate and feminine, and yet conscious of her opinions and loyalty to her Norman ancestry and the realm. *(Female, juvenile or twenties)*

DISHY DOLLY BROWN. 'Dame' with the usual frivolous and blustery attributes. Also has 'motherly' side, and 'fun' passion for Will Scarlett, but finds true 'pudding', love with the Sheriff. *(Male - middle aged)*

FRIAR TUCK-IN. Rotund, jolly character who likes his food. Follows the righteous life (?) yet has fun as well. *(Male or Female, middle aged/older)*

WILL SCARLETT. Somewhat quiet and reserved fellow, yet forever by Robin's side, until he meets Fiona. *(Male/Female, juvenile/twenties)*

MYSTIC MOG. 'Woeful' and 'Wondrous' personality part, with exaggerated actions and voice, and involved in some comedy. *(Female, any age)*

PRINCE JOHN. An arrogant nasty bit of work. Treats everyone with contempt, but can be a bit smarmy. does not suffer fools. *(Male/Female, middle aged)*

SHERIFF OF NOTTINGHAM. A right 'Bogey Man', and the subject of 'Boos', for his nastiness. Often a bit 'naff', as he is really a cowardly creep, despite his outlook and passion for Dolly. *(Male/Female - middle aged)*

PING and **PONG**. Stupid henchmen, with Ping the silliest. Do the nasty Sheriff's deeds, but involved with the comedy. *(Male/Female, juvenile/older)*

MUNCH. A realistic youngster's role. Likes to be involved with everything from action to comedy. No Prob! Scout's Honour. *(Male, youngster/juvenile)*

FRED. Plays large part, mainly in the comic situations and song and dance routines. Must be agile and prepared for anything. *(Male/Female, any age)*

KING RICHARD I. A staunch and upright character as befits a King. *(Male - middle aged)*

LOTTERY. Forever the 'Poet' and bearer of good and bad news. Dry humour, and always actions his words with wide sweeping gestures. *(Male or Female - any age)*

LITTLE JOHN. A stout and sturdy follower of Robin, and can be relied upon to do Robin's bidding. Has a hearty laugh for all. *(Male or Female - twenties/older)*

STINKER. A loyal 'Merry Man' who undertakes any tasks for Robin. *(Male or Female - middle aged)*

FEARLESS FIONA. A fighter when needed, protecting her friends, and yet has a very feminine approach to Will Scarlett. *(Female - juvenile/twenties)*

JULIE. A fun part. 'Guides' events with her Video control. *(Female, youngster/juvenile)*

HERA. Gentle 'Fairy Godmother' type role with grace and softness. *(Female, middle aged)*

LUCY LOCKIT. Must be real nasty at times, but involved with some comedy/romance. Preferably 'vampish', but can be 'matronly'. *(Female, any age)*

SIR GUY OF GISBORNE. Real 'Black Knight' very short-lived role. Can be played by either a very large, or very small person. *(Male/Female, any age)*

TIM/TOM. Small parts, yet latch onto Fred and Munch as 'Cubs'. *(Male, youngsters)*

ANNA/EMMA. Small parts again. Play roles of Dolly's 'Brownies'. *(Female, youngsters)*

SNIFFER. Dog who often barks. Involved in some comedy. *(Male/Female, youngster)*

TASTY. Fun part. Must be ready to be 'plucked and squeezed'. *(Male/Female, youngster)*

PENNY. A somewhat sad role, yet has some fun and finds happiness. *(Female - youngster/juvenile)*

PERCY. A 'bit' part, in search of his sister Penny. *(Male - juvenile)*

TWIT. Not a lot to say, but thereabouts for much of the panto. *(Male or Female - youngster)*

CHORUS NOTE: Players mentioned below are a mix of adults and children as appropriate, and act as personified.

MERRY MAIDS & MEN, SOLDIERS, CUBS, BROWNIES, YOUNG DEER, ANIMALS.

The theme of the Pantomime is to create laughter and happiness. When played with enthusiasm, both yourselves and the audience should enjoy it. And don't forget, 'Poetic licence, is yours to amend, ad-lib or 'Dib-Dib-Dib' as appropriate. Rousing family entertainment with song and comedy at its best - and worst!

MUSICAL NUMBERS

The songs included here are suggestions only for the type of music that can be used. Final choice is left to the Musical Director.

Please note that permission from **Jasper Publishing** to perform this play **does not** include permission to use copyright songs and music suggested here. Performers are urged to consult the Performing Right Society. *(see note below)*

Background music before Prologue - Legend style mix.

Legend. This song has been specially written for the Pantomime, and should remain. I hope you will enjoy singing it, and your audience remember it. Sheet music is available from the publisher.

The following statement, provided by the Performing Right Society Ltd., concerning the use of music, is included here for your attention.

The permission of the owner of the performing right in copyright music must be obtained before any public performance may be given, whether in conjunction with a play or sketch or otherwise, and this permission is just as necessary for amateur performances as for professional. The majority of copyright musical works (other than oratorios, musical plays and similar dramatico-musical works) are controlled in the British Commonwealth by the **Performing Right Society Ltd., 29-33 Berners St, London W1P 4AA.**

The Society's practice is to issue licences authorising the use of its repertoire to the proprietors of premises at which music is publicly performed, or alternatively, to the organisers of musical entertainment, but the Society does not require payment of fees by performers as such. Producers or promoters of plays, sketches etc., at which music is to be performed, during or after the play or sketch, should ascertain whether the premises at which the performances are to be given are covered by a licence issued by the Society, and if they are not, should make application to the Society for particulars as to the fee payable.

SONGS AND MUSIC NOTES

Suggested songs are 'popular' songs. Some may be old but are still catchy, and should be liked by the children, or remembered by parents. However, you are welcome to change any *(except 'Legend' - please see above)* as per local mood or ability of cast/musicians etc., and latest popularity scene.

A Pantomime should be brisk most of the time and often a song is too long to keep up the pace. It is quite acceptable to reduce a song to keep within a two to two and a half minute maximum. Length of comedy songs depends on your own specification, or the reaction or involvement by the audience so play it by ear. Within the script text, I have identified where other music may be needed, indicated as *(music)* This is at your discretion, but it is where I saw a need to enhance the atmosphere to the particular routine. Of course, you are quite at liberty to put your own music in at any time.

MARKETING AND PROMOTING

This Pantomime is based on the legend of 'Sir Robin of Loxsly'. When advertising 'ROBIN HOOD', or for additions to your posters/programs, it is suggested that some or all of the following are used together with normal standards of; Traditional/Romantic/Enchanting/Hilarious/Happiness/etc.,

Spectacular opening sequence of colourful Maypole Dancing.
Have fun with DAME DISHY DOLLY when she discovers that
TASTY, the goose, lays something special for FRIAR TUCK-IN!
LITTLE JOHN gives ROBIN HOOD a lesson in crossing bridges.
BOO the creepy nasty SHERIFF OF NOTTINGHAM as he exploits
the Saxons, until he finds happiness is Dolly's puddings!
Can MYSTIC MOG tell the future, or just 'Wondrous Wos'?
Hilarious routine as LOTTERY the messenger tries anything
to revive his faithful carrier pigeon - Bernie!
Join ROBIN HOOD'S band of 'Merry Men' when he seeks recruits
from the audience. A fabulous song and dance end to ACT 1.
Wonderful colour scenes, **SHERWOOD FOREST** and **THE
TOURNAMENT**
Watch amazed as ROBIN HOOD 'Splits' the arrow to win the
Tournament, the 'Golden Arrow, and the heart of a Lady!
Comedy with FRED as he saves ROBIN HOOD from hanging.
Tremble with terror when the King's wicked brother PRINCE
JOHN orders 'THE BLACK KNIGHT' to kill ROBIN HOOD!
Much excitement as MUNCH and 'Cubs', and JULIE with her
'Brownies' creep round audience to help rescue MAID MARION.
True happiness and romance as ROBIN HOOD saves Maid Marion,
and KING RICHARD THE LIONHEART arranges a 'Noble Wedding'.
For all the family. Lively songs, action and comedy in which the
children and adults can join in the fun - be part of a **LEGEND!**

*These suggested phrases do not give away the plot, but represent some
of the important aspects and routines*

Author's Note

Research for 'Robin Hood' was exciting, contradictory and frustrating. Where does a legend start? The earliest literary reference is in a poem by William Langland, in 1377, and goes;

> I kan noght parfitly my Patermaster as the preest syngeth,
> But I kan rymes of Robyn Hood and Randolf Erl of Chestre.

However, from other subsequent documents, and tales told, it is believed that Robin Hood (numerous variant spellings - Robyne Hude, Robyn Hode etc.,) lived between 1160 and 1247, yet one death record is 1198. Also, all the characters that now make up the tale, again a great many different names, (Scarlett was Scadlock, Scatheloke etc.,) were added at later dates. Maid Marion does not appear until the sixteenth century, and initially her name appeared to be Matilda. There is no real evidence that Robin was anything other than a robbing yeoman, peasant outlaw, who although using bow and arrow, primarily used a sword, and as appeared was true, he stole from the rich to give to the poor - his 'merry' band of men and wenches. But, as befits any legend, the tales soon took on an element of romantic bravado, together with the nobility aspect of being a descendant of the Earl of Huntingdon, to become a likeable rogue and rascal. In order to retain the tradition of the current legendary version of Robin Hood, I too have glamorised (humorously I hope) the tale, to present you with a pantomime adventure that we can all enjoy. Perhaps indeed he was as we now portray, for 'tis after all, the greatest and enthralling 'true legend' of modern times.

Dedications

Thank you Howard and Mark Southgate for the excellent music notation of 'Legend'. Thank you Brian Corrie for an admirable front cover.

Penny and Percy are for Alex, Michaëlla and Matt.

Robin Hood is with fond appreciation for Susan O'Brien.

Robin Hood

ACT 1

PROLOGUE

When all are seated, a Spokesperson from the Theatre/Drama Club enters and speaks the Prologue

Spokesperson Children, parents, everyone, welcome. Thank you so much for joining us tonight. We hope you enjoy the performance you are about to see. It happened in a time centuries ago, in olden England days when King Richard the Lionheart ruled. He was a goodly Norman king under whose rule the Saxon people fared well. The king departed these shores to fight in the Holy Crusades and left his kingdom in charge of a loyal nobleman. But King Richard's brother, Prince John, wanted the throne and was soon rid of the nobleman, and secretly planned his brother's death so that he could rule himself. Prince John's men imposed severe taxes and took the peoples belongings and animals. The Saxons became poorer as Prince John became richer. What happened then? Well, 'tis a tale that has been boldly told down the years. A tale of a man who fought for righteousness over tyranny, for his king and country over wicked oppression by the prince, and for goodness over evil. This is the story of that man, that hero. We give you a tale of that legend - Robin Hood. *(exits)*

SCENE 1

Sherwood Village, afternoon. Medieval village setting with 'ROYAL BOAR' (or local) tavern OPS with stout table/bench outside. Entrance to tavern via archway and PS, sign to 'SHERWOOD FOREST/NOTTINGHAM CASTLE'. Centre is pole round which children are singing and dancing 'Maypole Dance'. Stinker (Sniffer at feet), Fred and Friar Tuck-in are drinking ale at table. Mystic Mog (Tasty by side) is on opposite side with small table and her 'Crystal Ball'. Munch, Julie, Rob, Bob, Anna and Emma and other children dancing. Some straw about and bales for seats. Villagers seated/standing, join in song heartily. Chorus sing optional words or all. Carnival atmosphere for start of pantomime

SONG NO 1

SHE'LL BE WEARING PINK PYJAMAS WHEN SHE COMES

We are dancing round the Maypole yes we are. *(yes we are)*
We are dancing round the Maypole yes we are. *(yes we are)*
We are dancing round the Maypole, dancing round the Maypole.
Dancing round the Maypole yes we are.

Singing i-yi-yippi-yippi-yay *(yippi-yay)*
Singing i-yi-yippi-yippi-yay *(yippi-yay)*
Singing i-yi-yippi, i-yi-yippi
I-yi-yippi-yippi-yay.
Dishy Dolly should be here very soon. *(very soon)*
Dishy Dolly should be here very soon. *(very soon)*
Dishy Dolly should be here, Dishy Dolly should be here.
Dishy Dolly should be here very soon.

Singing i-yi-yippi-yippi-yay *(yippi-yay)*
Singing i-yi-yippi-yippi-yay *(yippi-yay)*
Singing i-yi-yippi, i-yi-yippi
I-yi-yippi-yippi-yay.
She'll be wearing pink pyjamas when she comes. *(when she comes)*
She'll be wearing pink pyjamas when she comes. *(when she comes)*
She'll be wearing pink pyjamas, wearing pink pyjamas.
She'll be wearing pink pyjamas when she comes.

Singing i-yi-yippi-yippi-yay *(yippi-yay)*
Singing i-yi-yippi-yippi-yay *(yippi-yay)*
Singing i-yi-yippi, i-yi-yippi
I-yi-yippi-yippi-yay.
Singing i-yi-yippi, i-yi-yippi
I-yi-yippi-yippi-yiyyy ...

Long last high note, chorus arms outstretched; all applaud / cheer. Villagers juggle, play music etc., and cheer ("Hello Dishy / Hello Dolly") as Dolly in pyjamas enters OPS

DOLLY Oh dear, so busy today with May Day games, haven't had time to get dressed. *(sees audience)* Oh! My goodness what a lot of children. Did you enjoy the Maypole Dance?
AUDIENCE Yes!
DOLLY Oh goody. *(twirls)* Do you like my jim-jams? Latest fashion you know, got them from *(local grot shop)* Anyway, I'm Dishy Dolly Brown *(poses)* don't you think I'm dishy? Could serve me up anytime! *(giggles)* Actually, I'm Maid Marion's maid but I've got the day off to help the children. We are going to have so much fun today, and...
MYSTIC *(looking in crystal ball)* Wo wo and thrice wo...

Stinker and others help clear the pole

DOLLY And what's the matter with you?
MYSTIC *(peering into ball)* I see bad times ahead...
DOLLY *(to audience)* Take no notice of her, never gets anything right. Bit like *(TV Weather person)* with the weather. She *(indicate with thumb)* is Mystic Mog the fortune teller; she's a catty person she is. She is you know, called me a silly old bag last week. Still, I was going to be a fortune teller once, but I couldn't see a future in it. *(laughs outrageously)*.
FRIAR Come on Stinker the tinker, your round.

STINKER 'Ere you are Fred. *(gives money to Fred, indicates to get mugs/ale)* He didn't earn much today. Nobody gets much money any more since those Normans came.

FRIAR And here's something for food, if there is any.

DOLLY Always eating he is, that's why we call him Friar Tuck-in. Eat anything he will.

Fred takes mugs into Inn as Ping and Pong enter. PS and pin notices to walls. General boos

Oh no, this is Ping and Pong, the nasty Sheriff's men.

PONG: Move aside there you Saxon Dogs. Prince John in London has sent orders for more taxes to be collected.

PING Him and his Barons can't live in the style they wish to be accustomed to. Bit like *(local dignitary)*

PONG For those that can't read, another three groats a week, *(sneers)* just to live, *(pause, looks round at frightened faces)* in your hovels.

PING Ouch! Pricked meself!

DOLLY There's no answer to that is there! *(or, 'We don't wish to know that, kindly leave the stage')*

PONG *(moving to front)* And if you can't pay, we'll be taking your pigs and chickens. *(spots Tasty)* We'll 'ave her for starters.

PING *(goes over, gormless)* No Pong, you 'ave prawn cocktail for starters.

Tasty cowers behind Mystic as Fred comes out of tavern, puts mugs down and follows Ping

PONG *(frightened)* 'Ere Ping, you got a bear behind.

Ping looks confused, and half looks then feels one cheek of his bottom

PING No I haven't Pong.

PONG Yes you have, you got a bear behind.

PING *(half looks then feels other cheek)* What you on about?

PONG *(hysterical as Fred approaches menacingly)* YOU GOT A BEAR BEHIND!

Ping feels both cheeks, then turns looking down, sees Fred. Slowly looks up to face him; both scrabble off into tavern shouting 'Agh/Help' etc. All on stage laugh, some gather round and congratulate Fred returning to table

STINKER Well done Fred.

MYSTIC More taxes. I told you, bad times ahead, I said.

FRIAR With King Richard off fighting crusades in the Holy Land, there's not a lot we can do.

DOLLY Well, it's about time someone did something!

Enter PS Will and Robin who dumps boar on table

ROBIN And we shall.

DOLLY Bless my soul if it isn't Robin Hood and Will Scarlett. *(to audience)* I like him that's why I call him Willy, I says to myself, Willy will, no that's not right, will Willy. I mean Willy will or will Willy kiss me one day?

ROBIN *(laughs)* Alright Dolly, no need to embarrass him. I heard there was not much food about so I brought this wild boar from the forest. Used my last arrow. Still, we came from the Crusades as quickly as we could after Lottery brought the message about the troubles here.

WILL King Richard will return as soon as he can.

STINKER But what's to be done in the meantime, Robin?

ROBIN Well, I know that Richard's brother, Prince John, *(boos from all, Robin gestures quiet)* has taken command.

FRIAR *(interrupts)* And he gets that rogue the Sheriff of Nottingham, *(looks about)* he's around somewhere, to do his dirty work. See *(gestures)* the extra tax notices from his henchmen just now. *(general mutters)*

MUNCH But Fred saw them off didn't he? *('Good old Fred' etc.)*

DOLLY Right children, whilst the men-folk get down to serious matters, why don't you take Fred for a walk in the forest, you can go via the meadows. We 'Ladies' will cook the meat. Off you go now. *(to audience)* Aren't they good children, just like those at... *(local school)*

Children go through audience with animals (Sniffer barks) As Tasty goes, Robin plucks a few feathers. Tasty 'honks' as each is pulled

ROBIN Ah, goose feathers, just what I need for new arrows.

Ladies exit OPS with boar

STINKER Here Robin, let me. *(takes feathers and makes arrows)*

MUNCH Can I stay and help?

STINKER Aye lad, this is what you do. *(shows)*

MUNCH No prob! *(does scout salute/wave)* and Robin, I can help fight.

ROBIN *(thinks/looks)* Well Munch, if you can fight as hard as your father the miller pounds flour... very well.

FRIAR I'll get thee and Will an ale, Robin. *(exits OPS)*

STINKER *(to Robin)* 'Tis not good news Robin. Those of us Saxons that cannot pay are tortured, some even murdered. Orders from that darned Norman Prince.

ROBIN King Richard's brother never was a goodly fellow. *(all mutter)* But all Normans are not bad. Richard is a fine and just King. *(pause)* But, he should never have gone to the Holy Land. He should have stayed to look after England.

WILL Well, it is you who must protect the people until he returns, and ... What on earth!

Commotion off as enter OPS Sheriff with Friar at sword point (hands up) followed by (2 soldiers?) and Ping and Pong cowering behind

FRIAR They arrested me. In the gloom in there, they thought I was Fred!

ROBIN *(laughs)* Understandable considering your size and ambling gait, Friar Tuck-in.

SHERIFF Silence! *(haughtily)* And who might you be?

ROBIN I might be... *(Jeremy Beadle/local similar)* but I am, Sir Robin of Loxsly, descendant of the Earl of Huntingdon, and who are you, that arrests a Friar instead of a bear? A buffoon? *(all laugh)*

SHERIFF Silence! You impudent scoundrel, Prince John will hear of this.

WILL Indeed he will. We will tell him. *(all laugh again)*

SHERIFF *(angry)* Enough! I am the Sheriff of Nottingham, and you will do as you are told? And was that not a royal boar I saw cooking in there? The penalty for killing royal game is death. Where did it come from?

ROBIN *(standing defiantly)* I shot it ... in the forest.

Munch has pulled Friar clear, and is threatening Ping and Pong as Fred also stands. Sheriff knocks him aside - boos by all

SHERIFF Out of my way child.

MUNCH I'm not a child, I'll give you what for, you...

He hits out at Sheriff. Soldiers grab him

SHERIFF Put him in the castle dungeons until I decide what to do with him. Lucy can deal with him. And as for you, Robin of Loxsly ...

Robin produces bow, takes arrow from Stinker, points it close to Sheriff's heart

ROBIN *(sternly)* I think not. And free him ... what say you?

SHERIFF *(flustered, pause)* Release him.

ROBIN There's a good fellow, now be off with you.

SHERIFF You've not heard the last of this.

'Baddies', exit PS to boos

FRIAR Thank you Munch, you fought bravely.

WILL Aye, but methinks with sword or bow next time.

STINKER And someone more his size.

Enter CPS Dolly, now dressed

DOLLY Come Robin, Willy and all. Fine pork cooked on the open fire, plenty of crackling. *(mischievously)* I bet Willy likes a nice bit of crackling?

All go in, Robin takes arrows, Dolly playfully pinches Willie's bottom. he reacts

DOLLY *(to audience)* It is good to see Robin home, he will look after us. *(thinks)* I'm often called 'Mother Brown', *(sadly)* because I look after the orphaned children after that Prince John has killed folk for not paying their taxes. Anyway, I hope Maid Marion is alright; she's gone to stay with her friend Fiona.

Sometimes fights like a wildcat she does, and she needs to. Lives at the Eastenders of Nottingham Castle, down Grange Hill in Coronation Street where the Archers and Gladiators live. Bit Sooty there and terrible Neighbours but she is by the Brookside. Can't remember, is she going out with the chap in Blue *(pause)* Peter, or perhaps it's Em..er Dale. Oo, and does her Heartbeat when she's on a Blind Date. But I know Marion will be safe with her, Home and Away. PHEW! Anyway, Maid Marion is King Richard's Ward. He's supposed to look after her until she marries, but as he is off fighting Crusades, and Marion can't stand Prince John, she's come to live up here. Mind you, we have to stay in the castle with that bogey man, the Sheriff of Nottingham. Oh, he's a right bogey man alright. *(excited)* I know, when he comes on, I can say 'Here's the Bogey Man', you can say, 'It's not, he's not". Is that alright? *(optional: just say "It's not:")* Let's give it a try shall we? *(gestures)* Pretend he's there. Here's the Bogey Man.

AUDIENCE It's not, he's not!

DOLLY Well done. *(repeat?)* Right, think I'll go and share some of Willie's crackling now. *(giggle)* See you later. *(titters and waves as exits OPS)*

Enter PS Penny who peers at sign, looks around, then walks through audience looking about, a little cry/sniff now and again. As off, enter PS Mystic and Julie to fortune table, and Tasty to some straw

JULIE Can you really tell the future, Mrs Mog?

MYSTIC Indeed Julie, come see for yourself. *(holds ball with 'Video Control' hidden at back, or up sleeve)* Wondrous wonders. Look, watch the mists inside as they reveal all. What do you wish to see?

JULIE *(thinks)* Um, oh, I know. What sort of fun will children of the future have?

MYSTIC Oh wondrous wonders. See, there is a square box in the corner of a room, with little people moving.

JULIE *(excited)* Yes, yes but how does it work?

MYSTIC *(holds aloft)* A sign, give us a sign.

Lights flash and percussion/pyrotechnic? The video control drops on the table. Both amazed as Tasty flaps and honks

Wondrous wonders!

JULIE *(slowly picking it* up) What is it?

MYSTIC I don't know, but look, *(poking it)* it has buttons.

JULIE *(aims at Mystic, presses)* I wonder what this does?

MYSTIC Careful now, we should not. *(voice goes down but she continues talking. Julie presses another one and voice increases to normal. Julie confused/excited)* and we wouldn't want that to happen would we?

JULIE What? *(wanders off interested in the control. Tries another button, lights go down. Then up after another button. Worried Mystic follows her and Tasty honks)* Why, these are magic buttons. This could be fun.

MYSTIC I think I had better have that. *(tries to take it, but Julie shrugs off)*

JULIE I must show my friends. *(runs off PS)*

MYSTIC Come back, come back … *(chases Julie off)*

Tasty honks and flaps as Dolly enters OPS

DOLLY *(Goes to Tasty)* What is the matter, frightened are you? Goodness, you must have been frightened. *(puts hand in straw, pulls out a round brown object, holds up)* What on earth is this? *(smells it)* Hmm ...

Lottery staggers on PS and collapses on bench

DOLLY *(puts 'egg' on table rushes over shouting)* ROBIN, ROBIN. Come quickly. Lottery has returned.

From tavern run Robin, Will, Munch and Friar

ROBIN Lottery, my good fellow, what's happened?
FRIAR Let him take breath Robin. Munch, some water.

Munch off to fetch. Others sit Lottery up as Mystic returns shaking her head

LOTTERY The... the good news, or, or... the...
WILL *(half laughs)* We know, the bad news.
FRIAR Let's have the good news first.
LOTTERY   King Richard fought in the Holy Lands,
                    The Crusades, they were won.
                    And peace will reign there evermore.
                    Beneath the tranquil sun.
FRIAR Some hope!
ROBIN And what's the bad news my trusty friend?
LOTTERY *(gestures with hand 'there's more, there's more')*
                    He travelled light to hasten back,
                    But in Austria he was waylaid.
                    King Leopold will not release him, till,
                    Ten thousand marks are paid.
ROBIN A RANSOM FOR OUR KING! How dare they.
MYSTIC Wo, wo, nay, lots of wos. I said bad times ahead.

As saying, enter Stinker and Munch who weaves through all carefully then trips, throwing water in Lottery's face. Dolly dries face with apron. Friar, thoughtful, wanders to Mystic's table. Sees 'object', picks it up, examines it

ROBIN Enough of bad times. We will collect a ransom to save our beloved King. Will, take Lottery for food and ale. *(to Friar)* How much in the church coffers?

Exit OPS Will and Lottery

FRIAR *(thinks, breaks off a piece of 'object' to the horror of Dolly)* Not much, and with exchange rates low, according to *(local Bank Manager)* we need a lot more. *(pops piece of 'object', into mouth, pause, then to Dolly's amazement, smiles and eats heartily)*

FRIAR Mmm... finest Christmas pudding I've ever tasted.
DOLLY CHRISTMAS PUDDING! *(goes over in disbelief)*
FRIAR Yes indeed, make some more of these, delicious.

Dolly shakes head, goes to investigate Tasty. Friar shares last bit with Munch

MYSTIC Not as good as my puddings, they've got special...
ROBIN Stop! STOP! I can't believe this. Our King is held to ransom, and you start to discuss Christmas puddings!
FRIAR Oh, yes, *(burp)* pardon. Right, let's go and see how much we have.
ROBIN Yes. *(shouts)* WILL, Will *(he pops out)* tell the men to sharpen their swords. Stinker, more arrows. *(plucks few feathers and passes to Stinker. Tasty Honks)* Munch, you can help. *(with purpose)* Little do they know it yet, but Prince John and that Sheriff are going to help pay the ransom.

Robin, Friar, Stinker and Munch exit PS

MYSTIC *(to Dolly)* Why are you looking under Tasty?
DOLLY Well... it's just that... I don't understand...
MYSTIC What? *(goes over as Dolly starts to squeeze Tasty)* Hey, steady on, that's cruel, leave him alone.
DOLLY Oh, Christmas puddings to you! *(inspecting Tasty)*

Both bent over Tasty. Enter PS Sheriff, Ping and Pong, Lucy cracking whip, and two soldiers

SHERIFF And what have we here? Two fine rumps I see.

Both stand up, turn and glare. Dolly points at him. Then to audience smiling

DOLLY Look who it is children. 'Here's the Bogey Man'.
AUDIENCE IT'S NOT, HE'S NOT!
SHERIFF *(indignant)* Of course I'm not, arrest her. I will not be insulted!

Ping and Pong grab her, and soldiers grab Mystic as she attempts to escape

LUCY *(cracks whip)* What shall I do with them your Sheriff-ship?
SHERIFF Put them in your dungeons, but first, where is that child who threatened me, AND, that Robin of Loxsly?
MYSTIC We're not telling you... you... horrible little toe rag.

Lucy takes dagger out, cracks whip and goes to pair, sneering. Enter PS Marion and Fiona

LUCY Shall I make them talk?
DOLLY Fiona. Quick, get help. Robin Hood is in the tavern.

Enter PS Julie and Fred

SHERIFF Good idea. We came to arrest him, *(nasty)* and that wretched child.
JULIE No, you can't arrest them. What for?
SHERIFF *(exasperated)* ARREST THEM ALL!

*Tasty flaps and honks at commotion. (sequence might take a while to perfect,
but should be hilarious. As each runs, knees up and exaggerated arms, all to
Benny Hill type music?) Tasty starts off around the stage, then around audience;
(OR, round and round in circles on the stage) Dolly breaks free, chases him*

DOLLY My Christmas Puddings!
SHERIFF After her!

Ping and Pong chase after them

JULIE Fred, quick.

Fred goes after Ping and Pong

SHERIFF Lucy, get that bear.

Lucy cracks whip and chases Fred

FIONA That's that nasty dungeon mistress, I'll get her. *(chases Lucy)*
SHERIFF *(to soldiers)* Stop her.

Soldiers chase Fiona. Enter PS Munch and Sniffer

JULIE Munch, just in time, help Fiona. *(points)*
MUNCH No prob. *(scout salute/wave)* I'll sort them out.

Sniffer and Munch waving sword chase after them

SHERIFF I'll get you, you, you young whipper-snapper!

*Sheriff chases Munch. Will and Lottery poke heads out of Tavern. Mystic and
Julie go to Maid Marion who is transfixed by whole episode. Having run around
the audience, all arrive back on stage and exit PS. Marion in centre, total
bewilderment. Enter OPS Will and Lottery, both a bit sleepy*

LOTTERY   We were tired and went to sleep,
                 Blissfully, with pleasant snores.
                 Heard a noise and thought we'd peep.
                 Indeed it was safer in the Holy wars!
WILL Well said Lottery, and what happened here?
MARION I am at a loss to explain.

*All go to sit on bench but then speechless as at back, all chasers run from
forest into tavern, followed by Robin and Friar looking perplexed*

ROBIN What's all the commotion? *(sees Marion, goes to her)* And who is this delightful maiden?

FRIAR Robin, this is Maid Marion, King Richard's ward.

ROBIN My lady. *(takes hat off and sweeps a bow)* I have heard much of you, but indeed, you are far prettier than they would have me believe.

MARION *(coyly, but proud)* And I have heard much of you, Sir Robin.

ROBIN All good things, I hope? *(laughs heartily)*

JULIE Robin, the Sheriff came with his men to arrest you and Munch, and then, well everything went crazy.

MARION *(to Robin)* Why would the Sheriff want to arrest you?

ROBIN *(laughs)* Oh, any trumped up charge, he is a...

Enter OPS Sheriff, Ping, Pong, and two soldiers

SHERIFF There he is, take him! *(draws sword, but stays back)*

ROBIN *(to Marion, draws sword)* I beg leave to defend myself, and, *(starting sword-fight with Ping and Pong)* hope to continue our, *(onto bench and table)* conversation under more convivial, *(jumps down)* and happy circumstances.

As above is going on, Marion is protected by Friar, and Mystic and Julie by Lottery. Will has drawn sword and starts to fight Sheriff

SHERIFF *(as fighting)* We chased off those *(lunge)* other Saxon peasants and a current bun stopped the bear.

ROBIN My, things have been happening. *(swirls in fight, takes on Sheriff)*

Will tackles others. Dolly with Tasty under arm runs in PS

And what stops you Sheriff, a...

DOLLY *(grabs ale mug and hits Sheriff on head)* Bang on the Bonce!

Fighting stops as Sheriff staggers around. All 'goodies' laugh. Sheriff's men help him to retire towards forest

SHERIFF *(rubbing head)* I will be back. You Saxons will pay Prince John's taxes. And as for you *(to Robin, sternly)* I will send for Prince John's champion. He will cut your laughter off... and your head! *(exit PS to boos)*

FRIAR *(afraid)* Robin, this champion, it's, 'The Black Knight', Sir Guy of Gisborne. A nasty piece *(quietly)* and I believe, he has a fancy for... *(indicates Marion)*

ROBIN *(looks, quietly)* And what of her feelings?

FRIAR *(quietly)* I think not.

ROBIN *(quietly)* Then there is nothing to worry about. *(loud)* I will deal with this 'Sir Guy', later, but for now we have far more important things, a King's ransom must be paid!

DOLLY I know, I'll fetch a bucket.

JULIE What for?

MYSTIC I know.

DOLLY Well you should, shouldn't you *(to Julie)* a collection from, *(to audience)* these goodly people.
ROBIN Good idea, Dolly.

Exit Dolly to tavern. Enter PS Fred, Stinker, Munch, Sniffer, Fiona, children/ folk. All go to appropriate places and excited quietly chat

STINKER Fancy accepting a bun as a bribe.

Fred hangs head in shame

MUNCH That's because you don't give him any.
FRIAR Should give him some of Dolly's Christmas puddings. *(rubs belly as Dolly returns with bucket)*
DOLLY I can't do a collection.
FRIAR Why not?

Dolly shows bucket with no bottom. Leads off with first line, others join in 'Well fix it, dear Dolly' etc., Song and dance, encourage audience?

SONG NO 2

THERE'S A HOLE IN MY BUCKET, DEAR FRIAR

Song ends, Robin to centre

ROBIN Lottery, make haste to Austria. Tell them that we will pay their ransom for our King Richard, *(pause)* somehow.
LOTTERY   But Austria is, *(emphasise)* another far off place
              And I'm tired from my last journey.
              (brightly) I'll send a message with my pigeon instead
              He's quick, and his name is Bernie. *(exits OPS)*
MARION Are you really going to help a Norman King? Yet you are a Saxon.
ROBIN Indeed Maid Marion, for are we not all people of this land, whether Saxon or Norman?
MARION Why yes, but you kill royal game, and avoid the taxes.
ROBIN Look around. These poor people have no more to give.
WILL Nay lass, Prince John has bled them nearly dry,

Enter OPS Lottery with cage. During below, he takes out 'Bernie' who appears dead. Lottery shakes it, massages heart, thumps chest, knee in back and pulls wings up, mouth resuscitation etc., Others ignore him mostly, until end of sequence. Lottery goes into tavern, returns with large battery with two padded electrodes, applies (percussion?) throws 'Bernie' in air, falls flat. Picks up and applies again 'Bernie' flies off (throw or fishing line pulled by offstage)

MARION I like neither Prince John, nor that Sheriff, and yet as a Norman, I must show some loyalty.

ROBIN Then show your loyalty to the King.
FRIAR Aye lass, join us.
MARION Well, I... *(looks at Lottery, puzzled)* What's he doing?
DOLLY *(casually)* Probably toning him up for his journey. *(goes and gives Tasty little squeeze/inspects)*
MUNCH Looks like he's trying to teach him to fly!
ROBIN Friar Tuck-in, for the time being, the ladies are in your care.
FIONA Fear not Robin, for I will sort that Lucy Lockit when I catch her.
MUNCH And I chased off those soldiers. No Prob! *(scout salute/wave)*
ROBIN Well done, but I believe the Sheriff means business next time. *(about Lottery)* What's he doing now?
FRIAR Looks like he's kissing the pigeon.
WILL Oh, back to normal, he's always kissing the birds.

All laugh

ROBIN Come on Lottery, make haste with that message.

Lottery off OPS for battery. Enter Penny from back of audience. Peers around unhappy/sniffs as all stop and gaze as she gets to stage, peers about then wanders off PS. Lottery returns

LOTTERY   I think that now I have the knack.
                     Please everyone stand well back.
ALL Ahh's! *(as 'Bernie' flops the first time, then 'CHEERS' as he 'flies off')*
LOTTERY   Bye Bye Bernie Bye Bye.
                     Fly up high in the sky.
MYSTIC *(watching)* Oh wondrous wonders!
ROBIN *(bit sarcastic)* Well done Lottery, about time!

Enter, back of audience, Sheriff, with Ping and Pong. Half approach stage

SHERIFF Prince John has declared you, Robin Hood, an outlaw, and confiscated your manor and lands. Sir Guy is on his way with soldiers to capture you!
MYSTIC Wo, wo, nay hundreds of wos. More bad times ahead.
DOLLY Oh look, 'Here's the 'Bogey Man'.
AUDIENCE IT'S NOT, HE'S NOT!
PING Yeah, you lot have had it now!
PONG Yeah, so sucks to you!

Munch, Fred and Sniffer (barking) make to chase. Ping and Pong scuffle out

SHERIFF And any more nonsense from you Saxons, and I'll, I'll put salt in your well! *(strides out)*

All on stage a little frightened initially, then laugh as 'baddies' exit to boos

FRIAR Come my ladies, we must escort you to the castle. I fear Mystic Mog may be right this time, *(to Dolly)* any chance of a mutton joint for the journey?

Dolly nods and exits OPS

ROBIN Stinker, tell all who would follow me to meet at, 'The Royal Oak Tree' on the morrow. Munch, take the animals to the forest for safe keeping.
MUNCH No prob! *(scout salute/wave)* Come on then. *(all gather about him)*
ROBIN Will, come with me to...
MARION *(goes to Robin)* But Robin, are you not frightened?
ROBIN *(laughing)* But no, are we not laughing... smiling?
MARION Yes, but this Sir Guy...

Enter OPS Dolly with large bone for Friar as Robin leads and others join in. All hearty and sway with gestures. Friar laughs/waves bone

SONG NO 3

WHEN YOU'RE SMILING'

At end of song, curtains

SCENE 1A

TALK TO THE HUMANS. Front of Curtains. Enter Fred followed by Sniffer, Tasty and Twit. All look around the audience

FRED 'Ere, that's a nice little one down there. *(points)*
SNIFFER Yes, and that's a pretty one too. *(points)*
TASTY I like that one over there. *(points)*
TWIT Well what about that one *(points)* bit tasty that.
TASTY 'Ere watch it, I'm Tasty.
FRED We know you are.
TWIT What are we doing here?
FRED Who pulled your chain? You're not even in this panto.
TWIT I am twoo... in the next scene.
FRED Oh right. Well, we've come to see the humans. They come to see us at the zoo and say nice things to us.

OPTIONAL, comments re 'feed us too, lets feed them' take sweets to children with Dolly (party atmosphere) ad-lib with lines below that she is the only grown-up who knows the animals can talk

TASTY But they don't know we can talk.
FRED The children do.
SNIFFER Yes, but not the grown-ups.
FRED No, but they *(gesture to audience)* won't say anything to Robin Hood or Maid Marion, or the others. *(to audience)* You won't tell anyone will you?

AUDIENCE No!

FRED *(repeat?)* There's good children/people, *(to others)* and don't forget, Munch said we weren't to say anything in front of anyone, *(emphasise)* unless it was an emergency. Is that understood? *(all nod)*

TASTY Mind you, if Robin keeps pulling out my feathers, I'm going to say something and it won't be nice! I'll get my own back later. *(to audience)* You wait and see, AND, I wish that Dolly wouldn't keep squeezing me.

FRED Oh, she's probably just being friendly.

SNIFFER Hey, we could have a laugh though.

TWIT How?

FRED I know, every time someone says twit, all the children can say 'twoo'. *(to audience)* How about it?

AUDIENCE Yes!

TASTY Oh goody, TWIT!

AUDIENCE TWOOO!

SNIFFER Well done. Who's a twit?

AUDIENCE TWOO!

Penny strolls on scratching her head. Fred approaches her

FRED Here's that penguin again. What's your name?

PENNY *(looks up)* Penny.

FRED And what are you doing *(emphasise)* here?

PENNY I'm lost.

FRED Ah, that's sad, isn't it? *(to audience)* Ahhh!

AUDIENCE AHH!

PENNY *(sniffle)* No signs for the Antarctic anywhere. Trouble is, I haven't got a map, and I'm a bit short sighted.

FRED Don't worry, we'll find a map for you.

TASTY *(comforting)* Yes, and some glasses.

FRED I got lost once. I'm a dancing bear and just love the music, but I couldn't find my way home. Shouldn't have listened to my old man.

SNIFFER Why, what did he say?

*Fred leads off, others join in. Stroll back and forth across stage with exaggerated moves and/or pretend instruments. Little shoe shuffle as appropriate. Encourage audience to clap and sing * lines, or, all song. Chorus behind curtains if required*

SONG NO 4

MY OLD MAN SAID FOLLOW THE BAND

My old man said follow the band,
And don't dilly dally on the way. *(clap, clap, clap)*
Off went the band with me behind it.
I slowed down as I... did a dance to it.
*And I dillied and dallied, dallied and dillied.
*Lost the band, and didn't know where to roam. *(clap x 3)*

*Oh! You can't find the band when you're hip and with it.
*And you can't find your way home.
  *No I dillied and dallied, dallied and dillied.
  *Lost my way and didn't know where to roam. *(clap x 3)*
  *You just keep dancing when you're hip and with it.
  *And you cant find your way home.
*Da da da da da....
*No you can't find your way,
*You can't find your way,
*You can't find your way homeeeeee. *(as music ends, all exit waving)*

SCENE 2

FOREST HIGHWAY. (Semi-forest scene with sign, 'FOREST HIGHWAY BEWARE LOW FLYING ARROWS'. Also sign, 'TO THE ROYAL OAK' pointing OPS. Towards rear PS an angled tree trunk over false stream. (NOTE, if players cross stream in front of trunk, they can tip-toe through pretending it is wet) Twit, is perched in tree FS. Woodland flowers growing, a bush, and birds singing. A little misty if possible, and lights lowish due to overhanging trees. Enter PS Hera, gracefully sings softly two/three verses. Sits on trunk with deer and forest animals to her side

MUSIC NO 5

ALL THINGS BRIGHT AND BEAUTIFUL

HERA *(breaks song, music fades)* Hello Twit.
AUDIENCE TWOO!
HERA Time for you to wake up.

Twit nods, flutters sleepy eyes

HERA *(to audience)* I am Hera, Lady Protector of the Forest. I oversee all that happens here, and protect all the little birds and animals, and of course all the children. Those that came from the village last night with their animals, they all slept safe and sound. But hark, *(sound of chat and laughter)* little ones, someone is coming, we must away. *(exits OPS)*

Enter PS Robin and Will, smiling/strolling

ROBIN Ah the forest is lovely. Fresh air, birds singing ...
WILL Aye Robin, though does it not worry thee that you are now an outlaw?
ROBIN No Will, but Prince John worries me. I believe he will not pay the ransom for his brother the King.
WILL Then what are we to do?
ROBIN First, we make sure all the people are safe from that Sheriff, and I hope *(thoughtfully smiling)* Maid Marion is safe too.

WILL   Oh, Friar Tuck-in will care for them, and I suspect *(laugh joking)* she likens to you too, Robin.

ROBIN   *(laughs/nudges)* Will, thou art a rascal, but she is indeed a fair maiden. Come, let us take a short cut. *(makes to cross trunk)*

Enter OPS a whistling Little John who places foot on first. Pause

ROBIN   Behold Will, a giant of a man.

WILL   Aye, perhaps we should make way.

ROBIN   *(laughs)* What! No, let us see what he is made of. Good sir, move aside.

JOHN   Nay, for it was my foot first upon this tree. 'Tis you who should move aside, and your fancy friend.

WILL   *(to Robin)* Let the fellow pass, for it is too fine a day to argue, *(laughing)* with an overgrown twit!

AUDIENCE   TWOO!

JOHN   Oh, I'm a twit...

AUDIENCE   TWOO!

JOHN   Am I? Then I will settle the both of you.

ROBIN   *(to Will)* Methinks a lesson perhaps in manners?

JOHN   If it's a lesson you're looking for, *(advances with staff at ready)* then come hither.

Robin takes bow and arrow

JOHN   You would fight with those *(indicates)* against a staff. Hardly a fair contest.

ROBIN   You are right, I will fetch a staff too, *(as cutting staff from side)* and we'll see who does the teaching. I like a man with the cheek of the devil, and the courage of a lion. *(advances)*

They cross staves. Following is spoken during fight with some blows landing. Robin an 'Ouch' or two. John laughs, then growls/roars

ROBIN   *(starts fighting)* He growls *(roars)* and thinks he is a lion. The lion... my fine fellow is king of the jungle... we will see who is king... of the forest... here today.

JOHN   *(laughs)* Your spirit... is good... and you learn well... but there is only... one king... and that is... my canny friend... the King... of our country ... good King Rich ...

ROBIN   *(stops and looks)* What! You follow the rule of King Richard?

JOHN   Aye lad, and the rule of fighting is ... *(thumps Robin on the toe)* don't stop.

ROBIN   OUCH!

John laughs. Robin holds toe, hops and falls off behind tree. John helps pull Robin up (see stage notes re; water aspect) OR, words from John to the effect, "Lucky you fell this way (falls to front) for the water is deep on the other side

JOHN   *(laughing)* A little water to cool you off.

ROBIN   *(laughs)* Aye, though lucky the spring is nearly dry and the brook low.

WILL *(to John)* No lessons for me thank you, you are too good a teacher, as Robin has just found out. *(laugh)*

ROBIN Yes, I feel bruised all over. *(rubs)*

JOHN Did you say, Robin?

WILL Yes, this is Sir Robin of Loxsly, known as Robin Hood.

JOHN *(excited)* But I was thinking of joining you. 'Tis lucky we met.

WILL Not lucky for Robin. *(laughs)*

Robin rubbing head and body, stops. All look at each other and laugh

ROBIN And your name, what do we call you?

JOHN My name is John Little.

ROBIN Hardly apt for your size, but from now on, for the 'little' you taught me. *(laughs)* I shall call you Little John.

JOHN What, I taught you a lesson in...*(sees Robin is being cheeky, laughs)*

All laugh. Enter PS Lottery, breathless again

WILL Why it is Lottery, something is wrong.

ROBIN Aye, so it appears. What's happened Lottery?

LOTTERY   The Sheriff is out gathering more taxes
                     With him are soldiers spreading fears.
                     And folk are paying what little they have.
                     For he has threatened... to cut off their ears.

Will, Robin and John gasp/horror. Lottery gestures with hand, there's more, there's more'

                     There's more to tell as I've been told.
                     And I believe it to be true.
                     He takes Maid Marion along as a shield.
                     To protect himself... from you.

ROBIN Then we must take back the villagers money and free Marion. Come friends, quickly to, 'The Royal Oak'.

All exit OPS in hurry. Penny enters PS peering about. Twit gets map from 'shelf', hops down. and gives it to her. Goes back to perch. Penny peers at map, then as if following looks up, then peers at the sign, ducks down and looking about, creeps off up highway OPS. Enter PS a flustered Dolly

DOLLY Oh dear, oh dear. What a terrible mess. Maid Marion being forced to go along with that Sheriff to collect the 'Ransom Taxes', Prince John's orders. *(now more brightly)* Anyway, I came looking for Munch and the animals. Have you seen them?

AUDIENCE No!

DOLLY Oh well. But look, I made this bow and arrow to defend myself. *(shows silly version to audience)* Those nasties might be about. Must get on. *(listens to voices approaching)* Oo, er ...*(scrabbles to hide behind bush)*

Sheriff, Ping and Pong (and 2 Soldiers?) enter PS as if riding galloping horses. William Tell music?

SHERIFF Whoa, whoa, rode like the wind *(as if pulling up reigns)* We'll water the horses here whilst we wait for the other soldiers guarding Maid Marion to catch us up. *(stops, Pong collides into Ping and looks down, realises)* Er, um, *(slowly)* where's the horses?

Ping and Pong look down/around, puzzled

PING They're... they're not here.
SHERIFF I know that, you Twit!
AUDIENCE TWOO!
SHERIFF Well where are they? *(Sheriff stands hands on hips as Ping and Pong (soldiers) dismount)* FOOLS!
PONG Perhaps we left the horses at home.
SHERIFF: *(exasperated)* Of course we didn't leave them at home!
PING Well, er...
SHERIFF We had them when we left the castle. *(thinks)* Do you realise what this means?
PONG Er, no.
SHERIFF We've been robbed! That's what this means. Robbed! My *(slowly)* what clever fiend could rob us like that? *(panic, then relax as pats pouch)* Thank goodness we still have the gold.
DOLLY *(jumps out, to audience)* Here's the Bogey Man.
AUDIENCE IT'S NOT, HE'S NOT!
DOLLY *(to audience)* I'll get his gold to help pay the King's ransom. *(holds bow and arrow wrong way round, nervous)* Um, er, get-em-up, this is a hold-up.
SHERIFF *(hands up)* What, this is highway robbery.

Ping, Pong etc. get behind Sheriff, arms up

DOLLY *(nervous to Sheriff)* Yes, this is a highway, and you're in a robbery. Come on now, your money or your life? This is an up-stick.
SHERIFF Stick-up madam, you mean stick-up, like stick-em-up.

Dolly drops bow and arrow and puts hands in air as others hands down. Pong picks up bow and arrow - gives to her

PONG Excuse me, you dropped these.
DOLLY *(sweetly)* Thank you.
SHERIFF *(to Pong)* You fool! *(puts hands in air)*
DOLLY *(fumbles, arrow waving about off string)* This time I mean it cock, your well and truly stuck up.
SHERIFF Not stuck up, more like a right cock up.
PING *(puts hands down)* This might be better. *(steadies arrow on string of bow)*
DOLLY *(sweetly)* Thank you, I'm not very good at this, my first time you know. *(threatens again)*

PING That's alright, I've never been in a robbery before.
SHERIFF *(clumps him round ear as all put hands up)* YOU TWIT!
AUDIENCE TWOO!
DOLLY *(nervous)* I'll shoot. I will. *(closes eyes and looks away)* Come on now. Oh, stop messing about. Gimme your money. *(drops arrow, twangs bow, hurts thumb)* Ouch!

All hands down as Ping and Pong help Dolly

SHERIFF *(amazed, hands on hips)* You three are a right pair if ever there was one! If you had any brains you'd be dangerous. Arrest her.

Dolly is tied with rope, to pull her

SHERIFF You nincompoops, you asses. *(thinks)* That's it. As I haven't got a horse, you can carry me back to the castle, like an ass!
PING But I don't think you're like an ass ...

Sheriff clips him round ear, then Pong stands at front and Ping reluctantly crouches behind. Sheriff climbs on, and 'whips' into action, swirl around, and all fall over tree trunk into brook. As clambering out, Robin, Will and Munch, with Tim and Tom (and Merry Men?) swing out or jump from side trees. Julie, Sniffer, Fred, Mystic and Tasty rush in PS. Fred sees Ping and Pong and chases them off OPS as Sheriff (soldiers) fights

SHERIFF *(shouts after them)* Come back and fight you cowards, dimbos, nincompoops, imbeciles... *(quiet as surrounded)*
DOLLY Thank goodness you've arrived!
MUNCH No prob! *(scout salute/wave)* We came to look for you.
DOLLY *(sadly)* And I was looking for you, and then *(to Robin)* I tried to get the gold for the ransom ... but it all went wrong.
ROBIN Never mind, you're safe now. We'll take you to our camp. *(draws sword and points at Sheriff)* And what have you done with Maid Marion?

Sheriff mutters as Friar, John and Stinker enter PS

FRIAR Maid Marion is safe Robin. We took the other soldiers by surprise, they had no chance.

Behind group, Ping and Pong run across the back of stage chased by Fred off PS. Sniffer barks as Munch notices

MUNCH *(laughs)* Hey look, Fred is still chasing Ping and Pong.
DOLLY Where?
JULIE Well, *(gets out Video control)* this little gadget has magic buttons, watch. *(presses buttons as appropriate)*

Strobes? Fred enters PS followed by Ping and Pong, all running backwards. As almost off, run forwards, then backwards, then backwards and off. All laugh as Sniffer runs about barking. Tasty "Honks" and flaps. Dolly looks underneath, pulls out Christmas pudding and hides it in blouse

MYSTIC Wondrous wonders will never cease.
DOLLY Magic Buttons indeed. What happened?
MUNCH Well, Julie was asking Mrs Mog about...
ROBIN You can explain later, we must away to the Royal Oak.
WILL And what of the Sheriff?
ROBIN Bring him, and his men along. We shall be hospitable, they can eat royal game. *(laughs)*
SHERIFF Let me go! *(mad)* I'll cut your grannies toes off!
MUNCH Hey, look.

Enter OPS Fred holding Ping and Pong by the scruff of necks. All laugh as exiting OPS

ROBIN *(laughs)* Come, a merry feast for merry men, and, *(takes pouch of gold to Sheriff's protests)* I'll take that!
DOLLY Come on Twit.
AUDIENCE TWOO!

Twit hops down and follows with Dolly. CURTAINS

SCENE 2A

A smelly affair. Front of tabs. Enter Ping with Pong behind, starts sniffing

PONG Cor, all that running has made you pong, Ping.
PING What?
PONG I said you pong, Ping.
PING *(smells himself)* No, I don't pong, Pong.
PONG Yes you do, you stinker.

Enter Stinker the tinker

STINKER You called?
PONG *(surprised)* No, I just said 'you stinker' to Ping as he pongs. *(holds nose)*
PING That's right, Pong thinks I pong.
STINKER *(smells Ping)* Ooo, Pong is right, you pong, Ping. *(then smells Pong)* Mind you, you pong, Pong.
PONG *(smells himself, awful)* Coo, you're right Stinker, I pong as well as Ping pongs. *(to Ping)* Ping, I pong.

Ping and Pong smell Stinker

PONG Aw, you stinker, Stinker. You pong as much as Ping pongs. *(gestures)*
PING Yes, Stinker, you pong as much as Pong pongs.
STINKER *(shouts)* SNIFFER, come here. *(enter Sniffer)* Ping and Pong say I
pong as much as them. Do you think that Ping and Pong pong more than I
pong, or do I pong more than Ping and Pong pong?

*Sniffer sniffs Ping and Pong first, then wines and staggers. Rolls on back, legs
kicking in air*

PING Ah, now we'll never know.
STINKER *(upset)* Never mind that now. Water, smelling salts!

*Ping and Pong get large bottle of smelling salts a cloth pad, and a 'heavy'
bucket of water. Ping applies salts to pad and places on Sniffer's nose, he
kicks faster. Stinker fusses over him*

STINKER *(perturbed)* What's in those salts?
PING *(slowly reads label)* Ping Pong pong!
STINKER What!
PING Well you said get smelling salts, and these smell.
STINKER Twit
AUDIENCE TWOO!
STINKER *(pushes Ping away)* Give him some water. *(looks in bucket)* Ugh,
where did you get that?
PONG From the... *(local smelly pond/place)*
STINKER You're not giving him that! Throw it away. *(helps Sniffer to feet,
staggers a bit and shakes head)*
PONG *(looks around, spots audience)* Ah, they look as if they could do with a
wash. *(holds with both hands, swings bucket)* One, two, threeeeeee... *(throws
nil content at audience)*

*Ping and Pong laugh, Sniffer goes over and pees on both from hidden squeezy
bottle. They stop and look down aghast as Stinker and Sniffer exit laughing*

PONG *(sniffing)* Cor, you pong, Ping.
PING *(sniffing)* And you pong, Pong.

*Link arms and sing, (off key?) sway, gesture with fingers closing noses and
poos. First on stage, then in audience before returning to stage? Amend the
wording below as necessary. Or, sing verses as appropriate*

SONG NO 6

WE'RE A COUPLE OF SWELLS

Oh we're a couple of swells.
We have the very best smells.
And people avoid us like the plague.

'Cause we're a couple of smells.
No-one has ever asked us out to teaaa.
As no-one ever smells like us no siree, no sireee.
We could walk up *(local)* high street to spread our smells about.
We could walk to Bucky Palace but the Queen would throw us out.
We could walk in the farmyard but there's smells already there.
So we'll walk in amongst you.
Yes we'll walk in amongst you.
Yes we'll walk in amongst you, it's what we like. *(pooooo)*

Oh we're a couple of sports.
Our bellies are out of sorts.
We haven't washed for over a week
And we haven't washed our shorts.
Mrs *(local)* has never asked us out to teaaa.
But we'll jolly well get back at her just seee, just seeeee.
We will walk up to her house and leave our smell on the mat.
We will walk up to her house and she'll pretend it is her cat.
Then we'll walk up to her house, and bring the smell back here.
And we'll walk in amongst you.
Yes we'll walk in amongst you.
Yes we'll walk in amongst you, it's what you like. *(pooooo)*

Possibly end here - out at back of audience?

Oh we're a couple of swells.
We make the very best smells.
And Mrs *(local)* avoids us like the plague.
'Cause we're a couple of smells.
Yes, we're a couple of smellsssssss. *(off with waves and 'poos')*

SCENE 3

SHERWOOD FOREST - THE ROYAL OAK. Forest scene with large oak tree centre, and logs for seats. Old bench/table PS, and boar/chicken roasting on fire OPS. On bench, Friar is sipping ale with Fiona and Marion. Dolly, Mystic, Julie, Anna and Emma are cooking. Tasty squatted. Robin with John. Twit on perch

ROBIN Well done merry maids and men...
DOLLY Yes, we all did our bit didn't we?
ROBIN *(laughs)* Indeed Dolly, your delay tactics worked well.

Enter OPS Sheriff, Ping and Pong, with Fred, Munch, Will, Stinker, Sniffer, Tim, and Tom. Prisoners guarded at back. Will goes to Fiona

SHERIFF You will pay for this, you upstart!
FRIAR Give him another hug, Fred.

Fred picks up Sheriff and hugs, all amused

DOLLY Oh look, 'Here's the Bogey Man'.
AUDIENCE IT'S NOT, HE'S NOT!
ROBIN *(sternly)* That wagon was full of stolen goods from the poor Saxons.
MARION But Robin, the Sheriff said they were to help pay for King Richard's ransom.
WILL A ransom paid with bread and belongings. Never.
MARION But you have taken the gold as well. Your men will squander it.
ROBIN *(takes the bag of gold from pocket)* Marion would have us believe that we are robbers too. Will you spend this on ale and fine living?

Shouts all round - "NO/NEVER/RANSOM"

FRIAR You do not know us well my lady, for ALL this gold will go towards the King's ransom.
WILL 'Tis Prince John who would squander it.
MARION But that cannot be true. King Richard is Prince John's brother. He would want to save him.
ROBIN A sheltered life you lead Marion, for as you appear to not know us, you know Prince John even less. Here Dolly, for your safekeeping. *(throws her gold)*
DOLLY I'm busy. *(hides gold down her blouse)* I'll find somewhere safe later.
JOHN I'd have thought nowhere safer than that. *(all laugh)*
DOLLY Cheek! Right, food nearly ready. Plenty of wild boar and mutton joints.
FRIAR And cock and cob? *(all look at him)*
MYSTIC Wondrous wonders Friar, chicken and bread there is.
DOLLY *(smiling)* And, Christmas Pudding for after.
FRIAR You are indeed a fine cook, Dishy Dolly Brown.

Dolly smiles and gives Tasty a little squeeze

MYSTIC WONDROUS GRUB UP, lots for everyone.

Mystic, Julie, Munch take trays of food around

FRIAR Come hither Mystic, and sit yourself down.

Mystic sits as others help take chicken/bones/food around. Will pours ale

ROBIN Will you not share food with us, Maid Marion?

Friar heartily breaks chicken in half, gives half to Mystic. (best if this is done with a real cooked chicken and loaf) He then takes loaf

Anyone like ends? *(looks round)* Well, Mystic Mog and I do. *(laughs outrageously as breaks loaf in half for each)*

Both eat and drink disgustingly and canoodle whilst the following occurs. Sniffer about begging on hind legs. Friar sees Marion hesitating

FRIAR Ah, perhaps Maid Marion is *(burps)* used to more pleasant surroundings, *(wipes face with arm)* good Robin.

MARION *(looking a bit distasteful)* Well, I...

ROBIN *(laughs at eating,)* Don't mind Friar Tuck-in tucking in, but, *(to Marion)* come Milady...*(takes napkin and small chicken leg which he passes to Marion who eats delicately)*

MARION *(looking around)* How can you all live like this?

STINKER What choice is there, Milady? Prince John drives us from our homes.

WILL And steals the animals, food, anything.

FRIAR But we stole it back, good eh? *(burps)*

ROBIN Indeed good Friar, but more manners please.

All continue to eat/drink

DOLLY *(goes to Fred)* What a good bear you are, keeping these in order. *(points to Sheriff)*.

MUNCH And us too.

STINKER I think Fred is fond of you Munch, and Rob and Bob.

DOLLY So it appears, like with cubs.

STINKER *(sadly)* Aye, but he hasn't got any cubs.

MUNCH No prob! *(scout salute/wave - brightly)* I know, we can all be Fred's cubs. *(thinks)* But because I'm the biggest and scout the forest... that's it, I'll be a Scout, and all the others, cubs.

JULIE I'll be a Scout too, like Munch.

MUNCH No, I thought of it first.

JULIE *(miffed)* Well, what can I be?

DOLLY Scout *(thinks)* well, search, guide ...

JULIE Yes *(excited)* yes, I'll be a Guide, and the girls can be... mm. what can they be? *(looks at Anna and Emma)*

FRIAR BURPS!

DOLLY Quiet you twit!

AUDIENCE TWOO!

DOLLY Got it! As I look after them and I am their Mum now, and I'm *(gestures)* Dishy Dolly Brown, you can all be my little 'Brownies'.

Girls 'YES/BROWNIES' etc. All children excited and gather round each other

Baden-Powell, we beat you to it!

ROBIN *(laughs)* Well done, Dolly, you have cheered them well.

DOLLY Now help clear up, then off with you into the forest to play. Scout and Guide, with your Cubs and Brownies.

MUNCH No Prob! *(scout salute/wave - organises others)*

Dolly proud as children help clear stuff, then with animals, exit OPS happily

ROBIN Come, let us show our 'guests' the rest of our camp.

DOLLY Here you are, *(dumps bits on Sheriff, Ping and Pong)* you can help clear as well.

Robin escorts Marion as all exit PS except Friar and Mystic, still eating

FRIAR *(looks up)* Cor, the whole lot's gone.
MYSTIC So they have mee dear, we didn't notice 'cause we were enjoying ourselves so much, eating and drinking, and, *(digs in ribs)* well, you know.
FRIAR Yes, well, I am a Friar and I have a habit, but... *(phone rings, takes out portable, listens)* Yes, yes, yes. *(different expressions)* Right, yes.
MYSTIC Wondrous wonders! That was... *(points up, Friar nods)*
FRIAR He said it's OK to spread a little happiness, with three 'Hail Marys' of course.
MYSTIC I was hoping to have big happiness, and you're mine. Those three Marys can leave you alone!
FRIAR Well, come on, let's go and get cleaned up. *(wipe hands on each others fronts)*
MYSTIC Will you give me a 'Fred Hug' later?
FRIAR *(questioning)* A 'Fred Hug'?
MYSTIC A bear hug, you cuddly twit.
AUDIENCE TWOO!

Both exit PS laughing as Hera enters OPS followed by children and animals

HERA Such a peaceful evening, and you all so happy with your new games.
JULIE I guided my 'Brownies' to you.
MUNCH No, I was scouting, and my Cubs' found her.
HERA Come children, no squabbling. See, *(gestures, young deer enter OPS)* you might frighten the deer. *(pause, all watch)* Would you like me to sing a song?
JULIE Yes please.
ANNA Can we join in?
EMMA And can we dance too?
HERA *(smiles)* Of course you can, all of you.

Hera starts off, all join in and then dance

SONG NO 7

DO RAY ME

Music ends. Everyone happy

HERA Let us return these little ones to their home. It is their bedtime soon.

All exit OPS taking deer with them, as Penny enters PS still peering at map

TWIT Hi Penny, no-one about, so it's OK to talk.
PENNY I'm still lost. can't make out this map. *(hops down and looks at map)*

Shakes his head and turns it the right way up, nods at Penny who peers at it. Twit shakes head again, and gives her his glasses)

TWIT Here, have mine, got a spare pair at home.
PENNY *(looks at map quite excited. As exiting OPS)* Thanks.

Enter PS Robin, Marion, Will, Fiona

MARION I think I understand now, Robin.
ROBIN I hope so, you can see the plight of the people.
FIONA *(to Marion)* Perhaps you should try to persuade Prince John to be kinder.
WILL That murdering so and so, he doesn't know the meaning of kindness.
MARION But you are outlaws now.
ROBIN That's true. The only way the people will survive is for us to steal from the rich to give to the poor.
DOLLY *(entering)* Well, there's no point in stealing from the poor is there, they haven't got anything. *(laughs outrageously)*
ROBIN *(laughs)* No Dolly, and we will have to pay King Richard's ransom, for Prince John will never pay it.

Enter PS John, Stinker, Merry Men, Sheriff, Ping and Pong

DOLLY Ah look everyone, 'Here's the Bogey Man'
AUDIENCE IT'S NOT, HE'S NOT!
ROBIN It is time to send these back to their castle, they have enjoyed our hospitality long enough.
WILL But Robin, they have not said thank you.
SHERIFF The only thanks you'll get is on the end of a sword!

General boos

ROBIN Methinks not. Stinker, *(looks, thinks)* what say you of these fine clothes?
STINKER Grand indeed, good Robin, the likes I've never seen.
ROBIN Then they shall be yours. Avert your eyes ladies, no peeping now.
WILL Aye, for it will not be a pleasant sight. *(all laugh)*
JOHN *(takes mickey)* Undress good sires *(to Sheriff, Ping, Pong)* a swap it will be.
SHERIFF *(protesting)* How dare you, I will not...
ROBIN Some help I think...
DOLLY May I...
JOHN *(laughs)* If you insist.

Strippers music? Dolly proceeds to help undress prisoners, swaps clothes to Stinker and Merry Men. Marion and Fiona peep and give 'Ooos' and. 'Ahs", and laugh with others. During re-dress, encouragement as required, Dolly gets mixed up wearing clothes with Will and Sheriff and almost undresses herself at one stage (keeps gold in bosom) She also pinches a bottom etc. All laugh throughout, with occasional 'Squeals' and 'Get off/leave me alone' etc., Sheriff ends up wearing bra outside

WILL *(about baddies)* How fine they look, like vagabonds.
ROBIN *(laughing)* Aye, Will, and how grand Stinker and the men are.

Stinker does happy swirl. Enter OPS Fred, Munch Julie, Sniffer, children, they laugh too

SHERIFF You will all pay for this with your lives. *(to Marion)* And you too!

Worried Robin goes to Marion

MARION Fear not Robin, for no one would dare harm me. I am King Richard's ward.
ROBIN All the same, I fear for your safety, perhaps...

Enter PS Friar and Mystic, jolly and laughing

FRIAR My goodness me, what have we here? *(pokes them on bottom, they hop about)* See, they dance.
MUNCH Huh, call that a dance!
JULIE Let's show them how it's done.
MUNCH No prob! *(scout salute/wave)*
JOHN Not for me, I'll guard these. *(takes prisoners to side)*
WILL Good idea, show them how to dance properly.
FIONA *(gets Will)* Yes. Let's dance!

SONG NO 8

LET'S DANCE

All sing and dance, some good, and some a bit outrageously. At end, after applause, Music Man breaks into 'Dirty Dancing'

DOLLY *(to Music Man)* Oi! Oi mate, cut, we've finished!

Music continues as Fred starts to dance

Oi! Cut, I said. We've finished! *(music stops)*
MUSIC You might have, but not him. *(points to Fred)*
DOLLY Yes he has, we've ALL finished! *(threatening)*
MUSIC Fraid not, he slipped me a fiver to do a dance.
DOLLY Oh, don't we pay you enough then! *(now off stage)*
MUSIC No, you haven't paid me for last year yet!
DOLLY Well, you don't deserve it, you're Naff anyway.
MUSIC Well, I think I'm *(we're)* quite good, *(to audience)* aren't I *(we)*?
AUDIENCE YES!
MUSIC *(to Dolly)* See, told you.
DOLLY Oh no he's *(they're)* not! *(in audience)*
AUDIENCE Oh yes he is! *(they are)*
DOLLY *(now threatening audience)* OH NO HE'S NOT!
AUDIENCE OH YES HE IS! *(THEY ARE)*
DOLLY 'E'S NOT! *(THEY'RE NOT)*

AUDIENCE IS! *(ARE)*
DOLLY 'IS NOT, S'NOT! *(THEY'RE S NOT) (threatens everyone)*
AUDIENCE IS, HE IS! *(THEY ARE)*
ROBIN *(laughing)* Stop, STOP, STOP! *(to Dolly)* You sound like the Bogey Man! *(to audience)* Would you like to see Fred do a special dance?
AUDIENCE Yes!
MUSIC *(to Dolly)* See, told you!
DOLLY Well, he's not doing it by himself, I'm dancing too!

Robin separates a fighting Dolly from Music Man and leads her back onto stage. Stinker gives Fred a Cape/Jacket and to front

STINKER Ladies, Gentlemen and Children one and all. I GIVE YOU FRED THE DANCING BEAR, ACCOMPANIED BY THAT RAVISHING, THAT BEAUTIFUL, THAT TALENTED, THAT WONDERFUL...
MYSTIC Oh wondrous wonders get on with it you twit!
AUDIENCE TWOO!
STINKER DISHY... DOLLY... BROWN!

MUSIC NO 9

STAYING ALIVE

Dolly showing off whilst above is said, then she and Fred perform the famous dance, with cape thrown offstage and back on again etc. All on stage clapping/ swinging to music. Big cheers/applause as dance ends (shortened version?) Fred and Dolly bow. Music Man throws Fred a bun

FRIAR See good Sheriff, even our bear can dance better than you. *(all laugh)*
SHERIFF You will all laugh the other side of your faces when Sir Guy arrives. *(sneering)* He'll be leading you a merry dance!

General hubbub of fear and some boos

ROBIN *(sternly)* Be off with you, and your men. I fear not this 'Sir Guy of Gisborne'.
STINKER *(frightened)* He slays all who stand before him!
WILL And he cracks nuts with his bare hands! *(cringes)*
MARION He is... I am frightened of him, Robin.
ROBIN *(apprehensive)* We will protect you. Little John, tie them and send them on their way.

John and Stinker tie prisoners in a line

SHERIFF And what of Lady Marion?
FRIAR *(to Robin)* I think Maid Marion should return to the castle until King Richard is released.
ROBIN *(thinks)* You are right. But send them and the other prisoners *(gestures off)* on their way now. We will escort the ladies back later.

John and 'men' escort prisoners off OPS

SHERIFF *(as exits)* Huh, I will get you for this Robin of Loxsly. *(boos by all)*
DOLLY Come 'Cubs' and 'Brownies'. Time for us to get ready for bed, we've all had an eventful day.

General moans as Dolly, Mystic and Stinker lead off PS the children and the animals. Robin plucks a few feathers as Tasty exits to 'Honks'

WILL What happens now, Robin?
ROBIN We have to pay King Richard's ransom, and I still fear for Marion's safety. I do not trust that Prince John.
LOTTERY *(entering OPS, breathless)* The good news... *(puff)* or the...
WILL Bad news? *(all half laugh)*
ROBIN Lottery my friend, the good news.
LOTTERY   An archery contest has been proclaimed
                A golden arrow and purse of gold to winner. *(puff)*
                And if I keep running about like this,
                Then I'll be a darned sight thinner. *(all laugh)*
MARION And what is the bad news, Lottery?
LOTTERY *(gestures with hand, 'there's more, there's more')*
                I fear that the contest maybe a trap.
                To lure Robin to Nottingham Castle.
                The soldiers hope to capture him there.
                That Prince John is a crafty rascal.
MARION Robin, you cannot go, it will be too dangerous.
ROBIN *(laughs)* What, and pass up the chance of a contest.
WILL Robin will win, he is the finest archer in England.
ROBIN Thanks Will, but more importantly, the purse of gold towards the ransom. Take these to Stinker, the finest arrows must be made and Lottery, take some rest. *(gives feathers to Will who as exiting PS)*
FIONA I will come too. *(off holding hands)*
DOLLY *(bitchy)* Flighty she is, much too young for him!

Lottery off behind them as enter OPS Hera. Goes to Robin and Marion

HERA I have heard of these troubles between Saxons and Normans, but all shall be well one day. There will be peace and harmony in this land, as there is peace in this forest of oak trees, beautiful flowers, happy birds and animals.
ROBIN You are so gentle with all your goodness. *(to Marion)* This is Hera, Lady Protector of the Forest. It is she who looks after us. Hera, this is Maid Marion.

They embrace. Hera looks at Marion. Soft music

HERA You are indeed a fair and lovely maiden, and I believe from the twinkle in Robin's eye, that he thinks so too.
ROBIN *(little embarrassed)* Yes, Hera, and I hope my feelings...
MARION *(shyly looking at Robin)* I too have feelings...

HERA Then do not fight them, enjoy them, be happy if that is your wish.

Robin looks at Marion and takes her hands

MARION Thank you kind Hera, for yours is indeed *(looks around)* a lovely, magical and wonderful forest.
ROBIN *(sadly but happy)* But come, you must make ready for your journey to the Castle.

They exit PS holding hands with Hera watching them. Penny enters OPS. Hera hears and turns

HERA Why do you cry so, little Penguin?
PENNY *(sniffing)* I'm still lost. I have a map and glasses *(shows)* and I went the right way, but ended back here.
HERA Let me see. *(looks at map)* Ah, you should have taken the left turning. Which is your left hand?

Penny thinks, looks at both, shakes head

I wonder if the children out there know. Do you?
AUDIENCE Yes!
HERA All right children, raise your left hands. Well done. How do you remember which is your left and right? *(ad-lib re answers. To Penny)* See, that is how you remember, now off you go. *(points through audience)* Out through the left/right. *(point as appropriate side to audience)* You will help her, won't you?
AUDIENCE YES!

Penny exits, deliberately going wrong to be guided by children, Hera watches and encourages, 'That's it/Well Done' etc., till out. Hera smiles and exits PS. Sneaky entrance OPS of Lucy and Sheriff, dressed again, to audience boos

SHERIFF *(peering about)* Yes Lucy, I was right, this is where we were taken. This is where those outlaws live.
LUCY You did well to remember the way. Ping and Pong would never find it.
SHERIFF Those useless pair of twits.
AUDIENCE TWOO!
SHERIFF They'd lose their own shadows! And these *(indicates audience)* out here are the ones who keep calling me nosey names, and booing me.
LUCY *(cracks whip, to front)* Shall I teach them a lesson your Sheriff-ship? *(boos from audience)*
SHERIFF Yes, whip them hard, break their little bones. No wait, you can deal with them later, we have come to recover my gold. You keep watch whilst I search *(sneaks off PS)* for that Dolly Bird. *(laughs loud)* Dolly Bird! *(laughs outrageously, then sneers)* She had it last.

Lucy cracks her whip threateningly at audience as John enters OPS and cautiously approaches her

JOHN And who are you?
LUCY *(turns snarling, then softens)* I am Lucy, and who fine fellow are you?
JOHN I am Little John.
LUCY *(laughs and smiles)* Why, you look more like Big John.
JOHN I have not seen you before.
LUCY *(thinks, then quickly)* I have only just arrived.
JOHN *(likes her)* Well come, some supper to refresh you.
LUCY *(hesitates)* But I am...
JOHN I will not take nay, come and join.
SHERIFF *(off)* Where is the gold?
DOLLY *(off)* Search me.
SHERIFF *(off)* Not likely, I'll let Lucy do that.

Enter PS Dolly in pyjamas with hands up followed by Sheriff with sword

SHERIFF I have her, search her for the gold. *(sees John, stops)*
DOLLY Ah, Little John, save me.
JOHN *(confused)* But what is going on?
DOLLY That's Lucy Lockit, the wretched dungeon mistress.

John looks shocked at Lucy

DOLLY And 'Here's the Bogey Man'.
AUDIENCE IT'S NOT, HE'S NOT!
SHERIFF Oh, I suppose I'll have to do it. *(holds sword down and with other hand, dives into blouse and pulls out pouch. Dolly quite likes it)* Ahh, nasty, but I have my gold. Come Lucy, back to the castle.

Lucy hesitates, looks at a still confused John, then in rush enter PS Robin, Marion, Will, Fiona, Munch, Julie ('followers'?) Sheriff laughs, holding pouch high, grabs Lucy and both rush off through audience or OPS. Boos from all

ROBIN All this commotion, What on earth has happened?
JOHN *(sorry)* I didn't know she was the dungeon mistress, and *(pause)* and the Sheriff got away with the gold.
DOLLY *(triumphantly)* But he didn't!
WILL Then what was it?
DOLLY *(to children)* Let that be your first lesson as Scout and Guide, and Cubs and Brownies. Be Prepared!
CHILDREN *(puzzled)* But we don't understand.
DOLLY I hid the gold under my pillow, and put some Christmas Pudding in the pouch ready for my midnight snack.
FRIAR *(shocked)* That fiendish Sheriff. He's got away with the Pudding, damn his hide!

Robin looks at indignant Friar, then starts to laugh. All laugh at the Friar who then sees the funny side and laughs too

DOLLY *(look at Tasty)* I'm sure there will be more puddings, you overweight twit.

AUDIENCE TWOO!

ROBIN *(laughs puts arm round Friar and Dolly)* Never mind Friar, and well done Dolly. *(more serious as goes to Marion)* Marion and ladies will be escorted to the castle whilst we plan for the contest tomorrow, and to make sure we have no further visits from the Sheriff, we need more to join our gang. Any ideas?

MUNCH No prob! *(salute/wave)* How about *(points to audience)* some out here?

ROBIN Yes, why not, good idea, good show.

DOLLY No Robin, not good show, more like 'Gang Show'. *(Or, 'Yes great, but you're the leader')*

Music and Robin starts off as others join in. Robin and lead players into audience as singing, and 'recruit' a few children into the 'gang' and take them back onto stage for final verse

SONG NO 10

I'M (HE'S) THE LEADER, MY (OUR) GANG

At end, curtains close then part open to allow children to be escorted back to seats. Should be a rousing and memorable end to Act 1

INTERVAL

It is suggested that on a Saturday night after the curtains close, Lottery is given winning lottery numbers, and emerges with Mystic through curtains

LOTTERY   'LADIES AND GENTLEMEN - NEWS FROM MYSTIC MOG,
AND IF THE LOTTERY YOU WIN - I'LL BE ALL AGOG,
THE NUMBERS THIS WEEK SO LUCKY MAY BE,
ARE A, B, C, D, E - AND NUMBER THREE.
NUMBER Z, IS THE BONUS BALL ALL RIGHT,
WE HOPE YOU WIN - 'CAUSE TONIGHT'S YOUR NIGHT!

MYSTIC WONDROUS WONDERS!

A slip of paper can be prepared beforehand with the appropriate message. The following are suggested

> The numbers this week will give you more and more - 4
> The numbers this week - so lucky may be - 3
> The numbers this week are no doubt for you - 2
> The numbers this week are both yours and mine - 9
> The numbers this week are a bit of a mix - 6 etc.,

Act 2

SCENE 1

NOTTINGHAM CASTLE. TOURNAMENT. Norman style castle OPS with entrance through arch and sign, 'TO DUNGEONS', A parapet above. Trees PS and sign 'TO SHERWOOD FOREST'. 'Royal Shield', on castle wall. Centre back a sky/ tree landscape with flags flying, and 'Throne' with a less grand chair each side, and benches at sides. Enter OPS Ping, Pong, Lucy with whip and a fluffing Sheriff behind. NOTE; see below for opening PS needed for 'Shot Arrow'

SHERIFF Everything must be in order for Prince John's visit.
PONG Looks alright to me.
SHERIFF *(wipes finger over throne)* Look at this dust. Get it cleaned up. Lucy, I hope you have a few Saxons in your dungeons to demonstrate our tortures.

Ping and Pong start dusting/sweeping

LUCY Yes your Sheriff-ship. One on the rack, one for hot poker treatment, and two ready for whippings.
SHERIFF Excellent! *(pause)* And if any get away, use these two nincompoops!
PING *(simple)* Thank you, Sir, dungeons are so exciting.

Sheriff clips Ping round ear, then shakes head as enter OPS a proud Prince John from castle

SHERIFF *(grovel)* Ah, there you are, Your Highness. *(gestures)* Final touches ready for the competition.
PRINCE Good. I expect all to go as planned. As you have not been able to catch this, *(contemptuous)* Robin Hood, I hope my plan of the archery contest works.
SHERIFF *(grovel)* Oh it will, it will. He is to be here, especially now you have raised the prize to ten thousand marks, Your Highness.
PRINCE Yes. Exactly the amount of my brother's ransom. All Saxon money *(laughs)* I thought it would tempt him.
SHERIFF *(grovel)* Oh, it has, it has. And so gracious of you to call a truce and bid everyone welcome, Your Highness.

Marion half enters OPS, stops and listens. Not seen by others. Ping dusting Prince and Sheriff

PRINCE I thought today should be happy, especially as Lady Marion will be present. We would not like her to see that I cannot be good to the people. And you will be nice to everyone. *(severely)* But, I expect you to deal with ALL the outlaws after Robin Hood is captured. Is that understood?

SHERIFF *(grovel)* Oh it is, it is.

PRINCE Good. *(matter of fact)* As we should not need him here today, I have sent Sir Guy on an errand *(pause)* to Austria. I don't think my brother King Richard will be returning to England, *(pause as indicates slit throat)* if you see what I mean. *(pompous)* Sir Guy will do anything I tell him. *(emphasises)* No one will stand in my way. *(grandly)* Do you not think I will make a grand King of England?

SHERIFF *(shocked but grovel)* Oh you will, you will.

PRINCE Good. Make sure the prizes are not stolen. I hear robberies are not your favourite subject. *(laughs)* Right, as I do not wish to see the children's tournament, I will now inspect the dungeons before going to watch my archers practise for the contest. Come Lucy Lockit, unlock it.

Laughs, but as turning to exit, sees a shocked Marion who quickly retreats. Prince unsmiling to Sheriff as Ping and Pong dust each other

Do you think she heard?

SHERIFF *(cautious)* Well, er, I, um...

PRINCE *(snaps)* You made more sense when you were grovelling. Keep an eye on her while Lucy shows me her whippings. *(smile, off OPS with Lucy)*

SHERIFF *(wiping head with handkerchief)* Phew! Prince John to be King! If he is prepared to kill his own brother, then if anything goes wrong here, what will he do to me! You two, stop messing about, and get more guards.

Ping and Pong exit OPS. Sheriff wanders pensively. Enter PS Dolly, Mystic, Fiona, Friar, Will, Little John, Lottery, Stinker, Sniffer, Tasty, Twit (no glasses, sits on bench) and Merry Men/others. Robin on, disguised, in background

DOLLY *(entering)* Now don't forget the truce today and we are here to enjoy ourselves. The Sheriff has allowed the children their own tournament. *(thinks)* He can't be all that bad can he, although, he is still a bit of a... Oh look, 'Here's the Bogey Man'

AUDIENCE IT'S NOT, HE'S NOT!

SHERIFF *(big beaming smile)* But I am, I am!

DOLLY *(to all)* See, he can be a nice little man. Oh, I think I'm going to like today. *(looks around)* I'll sit there. *(goes towards throne)*

SHERIFF *(protesting)* But, that's Prince John's...

DOLLY Now, now. It's 'be nice day' today, you can help me.

Sheriff cringes, takes her arm, seats her, then giving up, gestures to others to be seated/welcome. Mystic next to Dolly. All quietly chatting in groups

DOLLY *(glorifying her position with royal waves)* Is everyone ready? *(looks around)* Where's Marion?

FIONA I'll get her. *(exits OPS)*

DOLLY Come on Mystic Mog, whilst we're waiting, any sign of romance in that thing?

MYSTIC *(holds up ball)* Wondrous wonders reveal all. Ah, the mists are clearing, I see, I see. *(breaks into song)* One enchanted evening, you may see a stranger, You, may see a stranger, across a crowded room. *(starts laughing and points at Dolly, then laughs again)*

Others laughing at her antics

DOLLY What are you laughing at? Let me look. What is it? Who is it?
MYSTIC *(holds ball away, laughs at Sheriff)* I'm not telling you. *(loud laughs)*
DOLLY *(angry)* Come on, tell me.
LOTTERY *(sings to tune of 'Que Sera')*
                    Hey Dollyyy, Dollyyy.
                    Whatever will be, will be.
                    The future is hers *(to Mystic)* to see
                    And not yours *(gestures)* Dollyyy.

All laughing as Fiona returns with a somewhat nervous and fretful Marion

DOLLY *(composing herself)* Ah Maid Marion, come, sit here. *(gets up)*
MARION I must speak with... *(notices Sheriff who goes towards her then stops)*

Marion sits on throne. Dolly stands by her or sits next to her, as Ping and Pong return with two soldiers. They stand by Castle entrance

DOLLY You are just in time for the show. *(waves)* Let the children commence.

Enter PS all children led by Munch, with Fred last, on 'Space Hoppers' or riding 'Hobby Horses' or similar topical toys'. (mix?) All sing as a sort of dance routine, is performed

SONG NO 11

ON THE CREST OF A WAVE

Cheers as song ends and even Sheriff impressed, but moves over near to Marion Children take bows and most 'Toys' are cleared off stage

MYSTIC Wondrous wonders.
DOLLY Well done. Wasn't that wonderful Maid Marion?
MARION Yes, Dolly. But... *(nervous tug at Dolly)* I must speak with you.
SHERIFF *(moving in)* Ah, Lady Marion *(emphasises quietly but overheard by Mystic)* Prince John will be pleased that you enjoyed it, and, *(menacingly)* I should remind you, Sir Guy returns soon.
MYSTIC Wo, wo, nay a thousand times wo.
DOLLY Oh be quiet you twit.
AUDIENCE TWOO!
FRIAR My good Sheriff, when will the food be served?
WILL *(laughs)* I'd have thought you had enough yesterday.

SHERIFF There is none 'till after the archery contest.

DOLLY *(looks at Tasty)* Never mind Friar Tuck-in, there might be a Christmas Pudding later.

FRIAR Hope so, they're delicious. Did you enjoy yours Sheriff? *(laughs outrageously, others laugh)*

SHERIFF As a matter of fact I did, *(angry)* though it cost me a fortune! *(almost unable to control temper)*

DOLLY Why thank you. And Friar, no teasing, it's 'be nice day' and Fred, leave Ping and Pong alone. Right Munch, what have you now for us?

MUNCH Well, It's a special competition.

Suggest 'Hide and Seek' game to allow for a 'behind you' routine, and/or a mix with a game similar to one on TV (Gladiators or topical) Children can bring on basic, apparatus, and I leave choice to your Production Team of how played and by whom. Ad-lib as required with music of your choice. At end, possibly children off. Not Munch, Julie, Rob, Bob, Anna and Emma

DOLLY Well done, congratulations.

MYSTIC Wondrous wonders.

SHERIFF Yes, but it is now time for the archery contest. Ping and Pong, tell Prince John we are ready, and bring on the prizes. *(laughing nervously)* Better guard them, quite a lot of gold you know.

A few men get bows and arrows out to prepare. Lottery at side 'fires' a couple offstage. The children gather round. Marion still anxious

FRIAR Aye, a King's ransom I hear?

SHERIFF *(very nervous)* Yes, but, well …

MUNCH And there's the golden arrow.

SHERIFF *(relieved at subject change)* Oh yes, of course. And as it's 'be nice day' today, I'll arrange for prizes for your competition as well.

DOLLY *(to Sheriff sweetly)* If you weren't such a nasty old Sheriff, you could be quite nice. *(tickles him for a while)*

WILL Will you be entering the contest, Lottery?

LOTTERY *(shrugs)*   Friends, Yeomen and Bowmen.
                                    Lend me your arrows.
                                    For I shot mine up in the air,
                                    And they fell, I know not where.

Enter OPS Ping and Pong each with an arrow stuck on top of their helmets. They are carrying a small 'chest' of gold, with velvet cushion and golden arrow on top. All make way and laugh/point as they see them. Prince John and Lucy follow. Dolly stops tickling the Sheriff

PRINCE All this laughter, such merriment Sheriff. Indeed these are happy Saxons. *(to Lucy)* Perhaps we should have stayed here instead of enjoying your whippings and watching the archery contest.

All puzzled

FRIAR What do you mean, archery *(emphasise)* contest?

PRINCE Well, the children were enjoying themselves so much here, that I ordered the contest to take place behind the castle, and *(looks around arrogantly)* Sir Guy of Gisborne won.

Gasps from some and shouts from others. 'Not fair/What about us/No one told us' etc., Marion and Sheriff very puzzled

A worthy winner you will all no doubt agree.

General hubbub and boos

SHERIFF But I thought Sir Guy...

PRINCE *(stopping him)* Yes Sheriff, you thought what?

SHERIFF *(mutters)* Nothing, nothing.

PRINCE *(indicates prizes)* And you can take those away, Lady Marion can give them to Sir Guy later.

Robin emerges still disguised

ROBIN A moment, Your Highness.

PRINCE *(turns)* Yes?

ROBIN As we have not fired our bows, could not one of us challenge Sir Guy of Gisborne?

PRINCE *(thinks)* Mmm, we have a problem there. I have had to send Sir Guy on an important mission to London. But, is there one of you here who thinks he could better Sir Guy?

ROBIN I believe I could.

PRINCE And who are you?

Marion gets up, as does Sheriff, approaches to peer at him, others apprehensive

ROBIN *(slight hesitation)* Bernie the Messenger, *(bows)* Your Highness.

PRINCE *(inspecting)* Well Bernie, you may fire one arrow. Guards, fetch the winning target, it has been taken to the castle. *(to Sheriff for only him to hear, but Friar hears)* Go with them. Make sure there is an arrow in the centre. *(Friar now distracted)* We will now see if this 'Bernie the Messenger' is your Robin Hood.

Exit OPS guards and understanding Sheriff

Ah Lady Marion, *(laughs)* perhaps you will present the prize after all. Please, come sit with me, and clear a space there.

Prince sits on Throne with unhappy Maid Marion by his side. Others clear space from OPS to PS 'second opening'. Ping and Pong place prizes by Marion

JOHN *(to Robin)* We're behind you Bernie.
WILL Aye, make your arrow fly. *(general laughter)*

Guards return with target to just in front of PS 'opening' as Sheriff follows on. All gasp/point as they see arrow in bulls-eye

DOLLY Why, 'Here's the Bogey Man'.
AUDIENCE IT'S NOT, HE'S NOT!
PRINCE Quite apt, but well done Sheriff. *(pause)* Yes, Sir Guy scored a dead centre. Now Bernie, can you match that?

Robin looks and goes OPS, slowly takes arrow from quiver and aims. High anticipation from everyone, drum-role? Note, at this point, the 'famous legend aspect' depends on space aspects, ability, safety, etc. The final result ends as 'The Split Arrow'. (see stage notes for options)

ALL BULLS-EYE! /SPLIT SIR GUY'S ARROW!/HE'S WON!
MYSTIC Wondrous wonders of wonders!

All gather round and cheer, congratulate. Carry Robin on shoulders etc. Marion is delighted. Ping and Pong agog. Prince, Sheriff and Lucy outraged

PRINCE *(standing)* BUT...
FRIAR No buts, Your Highness. *(questioningly)* 'Twas as fair as Sir Guy's shot, was it not?
PRINCE *(angry, but then subtly)* Bernie fellow, come hither. Lady Marion will present your prizes.

Robin approaches, and Marion hesitates

Come Lady Marion, for this is, *(announces)* The champion Archer of All England.

Marion takes cushion and as presenting

MARION *(under pressure)* You are indeed a champion, *(pause, then confidently higher)* not just of archery, but of your loyalty to all the people of England, Norman and Saxon, and to your King!

Cheers all round, 'Aye' etc.,

ROBIN *(bows)* It is a pleasure to receive my prize from so beautiful a lady.
PRINCE Indeed, and listen to the cheer of the people. I congratulate you, *(pause)* ROBIN HOOD. Arrest him!
MYSTIC Wo, wo, nay ten thousand times wo. *(waves about)*

Rabble boo. Confusion (golden arrow falls on ground) all draw swords and start to fight. Prince takes his dagger, grabs Marion and holds it to her throat. Tasty 'Honks' and flaps. Dolly scrabbles around gets two Puddings, tucks into front

PRINCE Stop, STOP, or I...

All stop and watch. Lots of boos

Now arrest him! *(to all)* Lay down you weapons.

Ping, Pong and soldiers tie Robin as weapons are dropped. Sheriff and Lucy to Prince's side

Hah! Robin of Sherwood, you thought to get your King's Ransom. But, the gold is mine, and will be soon by right.

All puzzled as Marion half breaks free

MARION *(desperately to Robin/all)* He's right. I overheard. Sir Guy is not in London. He has gone to Austria to kill King Richard. Prince John intends to be King.

ROBIN *(struggles)* Away Lottery. To Austria, tell King Leopold we have the ransom. Little John, take the gold there and make haste. Our King's life depends on it.

Lottery speeds off through audience as Will, John and others grab up swords (or brooms etc.) and fight, some comical aspects. Fred growls but protects children. Sniffer runs round barking/biting. Tasty 'honks'/flaps around and 2 more Puddings 'tucked away' as Dolly also hits out. Little John/others get chest of gold but as taking off to forest, stop as Marion almost free, but Twit has hopped down from bench and peering about, gets in her way. Prince regains Marion, and holds dagger to her again

PRINCE STOP, STOP THEM! *(indicating to soldiers)*
MARION GO, GO...
ROBIN *(still struggling, then Twit gets in Robin's way)* Do as she says, our King and country are more important than we are...

Music starts, and all 'goodies' to front and sing (Robin untied?) as 'baddies' at back standing in line humming or joining in chorus. Or, as still in position and fighting?

SONG NO 12

WE GOTTA GET OUT OF THIS PLACE

As music ends, most of 'rabble' (Tasty stays) exit PS. 'Baddies' remain with, Robin (tied again) Dolly being tied and Marion who goes back to 'throat cut' position. Sheriff standing proudly by Prince

MYSTIC *(going off)* Wo, wo, nay a hundred thousand times wo.
SHERIFF Well, Your Highness, the plan worked.
PRINCE What? *(puts away dagger)*

SHERIFF *(confused)* Well, we captured Robin Hood.
PRINCE Yes, but they also got away with the gold, TWIT!
AUDIENCE TWOO!
MARION Oh, Robin, I'm sorry. I couldn't warn you before.
ROBIN Milady, it is not your fault. But at least you now know that Prince John
is a murdering...
PRINCE SILENCE! *(throws Marion to Sheriff and slaps Robin's face)*

Remaining few 'rabble' boo and hiss

SHERIFF *(throws Marion to Pong)* And this is for the trouble you've caused.

*Goes to slap Robin who moves head. Sheriff goes flying'. Scrabbles up as
'rabble' laugh*

PRINCE ENOUGH! Disperse this rabble. *(rabble sent off PS)* Take Lady Marion
and her maid and lock them in the tower. And as for him, *(Robin)* take him to
the dungeons for a whipping until I decide what to do.

As Lucy, Ping and Pong escort off OPS

PING Pong, why does Robin go to the dungeons, and not me?
SHERIFF Twit!

Sheriff clips Ping's ear as exiting with prisoners. Prince follows behind

AUDIENCE TWOO!
PRINCE And as for you, you bumbling Sheriff. I don't think you will be for
much longer! *(rages)* Ten Thousand Marks!

Boos as off, then enter PS Penny, looks about

PENNY *(to front/audience)* Quiet in here tonight, isn't it?

*Turns, sees golden arrow. Picks up and uses as map pointer, exits OPS. Munch
and Julie enter PS*

MUNCH We weren't very prepared for that were we?
JULIE No, and as for that silly brown owl forgetting her glasses. Getting in
Marion's and Robin's way like that, dopey Twit!
AUDIENCE TWOO!
MUNCH Well, he didn't mean it. Anyway, we've got to do something... Shsh,
someone's coming. Quick, hide.

Both look around, then hide behind throne

PRINCE *(enters OPS)* That's right, bring him up here. *(wanders, thinking then
sits on throne)*

Sheriff Lucy, Ping & Pong enter OPS with Robin in chains

PRINCE Robin of Loxsly, I have already stripped you of title, manor and lands, and now I intend to strip you of your life! You are guilty of Stealing Taxes, Inciting Rebellion, Poaching Royal Game, and High Treason to the Realm.
ROBIN *(defiantly)* Not the King's Realm.
PRINCE Silence! It is a pity about your misplaced loyalty, you would have made a fine King's Champion for me.
SHERIFF And, Your Highness, he has a fancy for the Lady Marion.
PRINCE Yes, but she will wed Sir Guy. Robin of Loxsly, I have decided you will be hung as soon as possible. *(to Sheriff)* Make the arrangements, and take him back to the dungeons...
PING Can I go too?

Sheriff clips him round ear

PRINCE *(to Sheriff)* I shall prepare for my journey to London after the hanging.

All exit OPS as Munch and Julie emerge

MUNCH Robin to be hung!
JULIE And Maid Marion to be married to Sir Guy
MUNCH We must save Robin somehow, do something. *(thinks)*
JULIE Yes, but what? The 'Cubs and Brownies' can help, *(pause)* and Fred of course, this is an emergency.
MUNCH *(brightly)* Brilliant! That's it! An emergency. Quick, go and find Fred, I've got a plan.
JULIE What is it?
MUNCH I'll tell you later. Quick, find him, I'll be with you in a minute.

Julie rushes off PS

MUNCH *(to audience)* Will you help to save Robin?
AUDIENCE YES!
MUNCH Great. Now I'm going to give Fred a bow and arrow. With one shot he can free Robin, but he might not be able to hear me tell him when, as he will be hidden. So when I shout 'SHOOT NOW FRED', you shout as well. Is that OK?
AUDIENCE YES!
MUNCH Right, quick try - 'SHOOT NOW FRED'.
AUDIENCE SHOOT NOW FRED!
MUNCH Great! *(as leaving PS)* Now don't forget, as loud as you can. Must find Friar Tuck-in as well.

Rushes off PS. Ping and Pong enter OPS with pieces of 'gallows' to erect. The end result must be quite sturdy, but a simple yet complicated, structure being built by idiots, should be fun, especially when Ping nearly hangs himself. Ad-lib, 'This way up fool/When I nod my head, hit it/Hold it upright/You Twit!/Tie a knot in it' etc., Both worn out as enter OPS Sheriff eating. Dolly follows

DOLLY Here's the 'Bogey Man'
AUDIENCE IT'S NOT, HE'S NOT!
SHERIFF *(smiles to audience)* I am, I am. *(winks)* Nice day today. *(to Dolly)* This really is an exceedingly good Christmas Pudding, just like... *(Mrs Kipperling/local bakery)* makes.
DOLLY I'm glad you like it. A little more for a little favour?
SHERIFF Yes, well, I shouldn't really, but what is it?
DOLLY Let Maid Marion see Robin, just for a moment or two.
SHERIFF *(uncomfortable)* I don't think I should.
DOLLY *(coyly)* Oh, It is still 'be nice day' isn't it?
SHERIFF Yes, but I don't think Prince John would like it.
DOLLY *(sweetly)* Prince John isn't going to get it.
SHERIFF Perhaps then, just for a short while, *(pause)* as Robin won't be with us much longer.
DOLLY *(puzzled)* What do you mean?
SHERIFF Er, Prince John has decided to...
DOLLY *(bribing)* Now Sheriff, more Christmas Pudding?
SHERIFF *(jolly)* Well, just a little then.
DOLLY You are a sweetie really. *(nudges up to him)*
SHERIFF Well. I er. You haven't got a secret supply in, *(points sort of nervous)* in, in there, where I thought the gold was... have you?
DOLLY *(coyly)* OH Sheriff. You are naughty, *(digs in ribs)* but I like you.

Sheriff moves closer to Dolly as she leads off. Enter Munch and Julie PS with children and animals except Fred. Song and rock dance routine

SONG NO 13

SHAKIN' ALL OVER

Music ends. Dolly with Sheriff to centre. Enter PS Mystic, Will etc.,. Not Friar

FRIAR We came to see what was happening
DOLLY *(to Sheriff)* We are about to find out. Now Sheriff, what were you saying Prince John had decided to do?
SHERIFF Well, er... *(hesitates)*
JULIE To hang Robin!

Gasps all round

DOLLY WHAT!
MUNCH Hang Robin, look, the gallows are already erected.

SHERIFF Ah, you're that wretched urchin who... *(goes to grab)*
JULIE And Maid Marion is to be married to Sir Guy.
DOLLY *(starts to bash Sheriff)* Never. And I was beginning to like you, you...
SHERIFF *(staving off blows)* It was Prince John, Not me.
MUNCH It's no prob, Dolly, we are going to save Robin.
DOLLY But how?
MUNCH *(secretive)* No prob! *(salute/wave)* We have a plan.

Enter OPS Prince holding dagger, and dragging a frightened Marion by arm. All boo and hiss

PRINCE Ah, there you are Sheriff. I have brought Lady Marion to see *(contemptuous)* her Robin Hood hung. Fetch him. And you his 'Merry Men' *(laughs)* we'll see how merry they are when your 'Hero' is hung!
SHERIFF But...
PRINCE FETCH HIM NOW! *(drags Marion and sits on 'throne' with Marion next to him)*
SHERIFF *(shouts to off)* PING, PONG, bring the prisoner here.
PRINCE And in case there are any more disturbances... *(points dagger towards Marion)*

Ping, Pong, Lucy (soldiers?) enter OPS with Robin. Funeral March or similar as Robin is lead to gallows. Friar enters PS, and a large box sort of shuffles in slowly hiding behind him. Marion terrified and 'rabble' heckle and boo

MYSTIC Wo wo, nay a million times wo.
DOLLY Somebody do something!

The noose is put around Robin's neck, and the box shuffles closer to gallows

MARION *(pleads)* Please, PLEASE. I will marry Sir Guy if you let Robin go.

All agitated, but guards and threatening move by Prince to Marion with dagger stops any action

PRINCE *(laughs at all)* Say good-bye to your beloved 'Robin Hood'. Prepare to hang him.

As Sheriff is about to pull lever for trap-door like 'Hunchback of Notre Dame'

MUNCH SHOOT NOW FRED!
AUDIENCE SHOOT NOW FRED!

Sheriff looks round wondering what is going on

MUNCH *(encourages audience)* He didn't hear - SHOOT NOW FRED!
AUDIENCE SHOOT NOW FRED!
PRINCE *(to Sheriff)* HANG HIM!

MUNCH Before it's too late, louder - SHOOT NOW FRED!
AUDIENCE SHOOT NOW FRED!

*The top of the box flies open/off and Fred springs out. (pyrotechnic?) He has
bow and arrow. Holds it with arrow pointing directly at his own heart (or head)
Cubs and Brownies guard him*

FRED STOP! Don't hang Robin, OR the bear gets it!

All look at Fred flabbergasted

I mean it. Let him free, or I'll kill myself. *(to animals)* Sorry mates, but Munch
said he had an emergency. Come on now free him, or I shoot.
ANIMALS That's alright mate/we're behind you etc.,

*Lucy (soldiers?) move in on Fred, as Ping and Pong cower behind. Repulsed by
Cubs and Brownies*

SHERIFF Don't anybody do anything, I think the bear means it.
PRINCE *(slowly standing)* He wouldn't dare, he's bluffing.
FRED I'm not. Come on now, or I'll shoot myself.

Cries of, 'NO, NO, DON'T DO IT FRED'

SHERIFF I think we had better do as he says.
PRINCE Fools! He wouldn't dare.
FRED I will, I mean it. *(threatens himself)* Agh, Agh, quick, do as the bear says,
I don't want to die.
SHERIFF *(half releases Robin)* We won't let you. Here, look, I'm letting him go.
(starts to free Robin)
FRED *(threatens himself)* Help! Agh! Don't shoot!

Ping and Pong help release Robin

SHERIFF Quick, or the RSPCA might get to hear of this, then we'd be in trouble.

All aside. Fred escorts Robin away (in box?) from gallows. Marion joins them

PRINCE *(standing flabbergasted, hands on hips)* I can't believe it, Robin Hood's
got away. I can't stand any more of this nonsense. *(to Sheriff)* You failed you
blundering... You're fired as Sheriff of Nottingham.

All boo and hiss as Prince storms off OPS

SHERIFF *(follows him, protesting)* But, but, Your Highness...

Dolly looks sadly at exiting Sheriff. Ping and Pong look nervous as they and soldiers slowly (Lucy in front, cracking whip) back off OPS to boos. Big cheers, "Saved the Day Fred" etc., as Robin thanks Fred, Munch, Julie etc. and hugs Marion. Fred is lifted on shoulders, all sing (half way into audience and back?)

SONG NO 14

FOR HE'S A JOLLY GOOD FELLOW

At end of song, curtains

SCENE 2

DAME'S DELIGHT. Front Curtains. Dolly wanders on. Large boobs, water filled balloons

DOLLY I wonder what Mystic Mog saw in her ball, and who was it. I don't think I'll find romance now. Will and Fiona are an item. *(topical)* Still, *(pensive)* I've got all my orphaned little children, I'll be their mum forever. *(happy)* I remember my mum, very small she was, I called her 'mini-mum'. *(brightly)* Who wants a man anyway? *(pause, cries out)* I DO! *(cries)*

Enter Julie and all Brownies. Munch and Cubs if needed/appropriate

JULIE What's the matter Dolly?
DOLLY *(wipes eyes)* Oh nothing… nothing.
ANNA But there must be Mummy, dearest.
EMMA Here *(gives handkerchief)* wipe your eyes.
JULIE What is it?
DOLLY *(drying eyes)* Well, I was thinking about what Mystic Mog said when I asked her about romance, and …
JULIE Oh, is that all.
DOLLY *(surprised)* Is that all!
EMMA Yes, we'll fix it for you to be on… *(Blind Date or topical)*
ANNA Yes, you'll be the first to be picked.
MUSIC More like the last!

All glare at him

JULIE Anyway, this is an enchanted evening, and look here. *(indicates audience, excited)* Mystic said a 'crowded room', there may be …
ANNA *(peering, points at back excited)* Yes, look!
EMMA *(peering, points)* See, a stranger.

At back, Sheriff approaches stage wearing hooded cloak, sings

SHERIFF *(off key?)* I am calling you oou oou oou…

All looking. Dolly points at herself, and sings, 'Who me?'

DOLLY *(off key?)* You are calling mee eee eee eee...
SHERIFF *(to stage)* Will you answer truee uee uee.. uee...
DOLLY Not until I can seee eee eee eee... *(breaks off)* Oh, it's you, the *(emphasise)* Ex-Sheriff of Nottingham. *(to audience)* Look everyone 'Here's the Bogey Man'
AUDIENCE IT'S NOT, HE'S NOT!
DOLLY Anyway, what's your game?
SHERIFF Well, I got to quite like to you on 'Be Nice day', and I thought.
DOLLY *(up to him)* You're not after my puddings, are you?
SHERIFF Well, er, I, they do... sort of... come into it, but...
DOLLY That's alright then.
JULIE He is quite sweet, Dolly.
ANNA I quite like him now.
EMMA You won't be nasty any more will you?
SHERIFF Of course not, and I was trying to say, as it's your birthday, I've brought you a little...
DOLLY Alright then, you smoothie, you've pulled me. *(OR 'I'M YOURS')*

All children jump happily as Dolly takes gift

ANNA We didn't know it was your birthday.
JULIE We haven't got a proper present, but you can have this. *(gives her the 'Video Control,', excited)* It does have magic buttons.
DOLLY Thank you. *(clutches both presents to bosom, happy)* Thank you. What a wonderful birthday.
EMMA *(to Sheriff)* How did you know?
SHERIFF Mystic Mog told me!
DOLLY If I am to be yours, you'll have to get your job back. Can't support all these *(gestures)* little ones without a job.
SHERIFF I will, I will. I'll look after you, do anything for you. I'd even fly 'Over the Moon' for you.
DOLLY You don't have to go that far. *(thinks)* But no job, no puddings!
SHERIFF *(confident)* I'll go and ask Prince John for my Sheriff-ship back. But I won't grovel, I'll demand my job back. No nonsense, I'll tell him straight. You just wait and see if I don't!
DOLLY *(flings arms round him)* I'm so happy, I could sing.
SHERIFF And I could be 'The Boogie Bogey Man'

All laugh

JULIE Well come on, Dishy Dolly Mother Brown, let's have a knees up.

All in line across stage, couple in middle

SONG NO 15

KNEES UP MOTHER BROWN

Knees up Mother Brown, Knees up Mother Brown.
Come along dearie let it go, Ee-i-ee-i-ee-i-oh.
It's your blooming birthday, let's wake up the town.
So knees up, knees up, don't get the breeze up.
Knees up Mother Brown.
Oh my, what a rotten song, what a rotten song, what a rotten song,
Oh my what a rotten song, What a rotten singer too..oo.

Repeat as required and get audience to join in? *Or, suggest 'couple' lead off, and others follow out through audience, getting them to sing as well. Care: Sheriff on at opening of next scene*

SCENE 3

NOTTINGHAM CASTLE - THE RESCUE. Castle as before but arch has doors. Signs to 'THRONE ROOM' and 'DUNGEONS'. Also, sign PS to 'SHERWOOD FOREST'. Flag flying by parapet, with rope hanging down to ground, and benches at sides. Enter OPS Prince with Sheriff dragging along holding him, followed by Pong, then Ping tugging on Sheriff

SHERIFF *(grovel)* Please, PLEASE Your Highness-ship, I must have my job back.
PRINCE Get off, leave me alone. *(thinks, still dragging)* Where is Sir Guy? He must have killed King Richard by now. *(shakes at Sheriff)* Get off.
SHERIFF Please Your Highness-ship, what about my Sheriff-ship!
PRINCE *(ignores)* And when Sir Guy returns *(contemptuous)* he will take care of that Robin Hood once and for all!
SHERIFF I have lots of children to support, and my lady love said, 'no job, no puddings'. Please *(grovel)* PLEASE!
PRINCE Get off. You heard me, have you no dignity?
SHERIFF No, *(brightly)* but I've got a little Christmas Pudding left, you can have that.
PONG No, we want that.
PING I don't. I want to visit Lucy's dungeons.
PRINCE Get off, Get Off, GET OFF!
SHERIFF Well, if you're going to be like that about it.

Lets go, Prince falls flat. Pong collides onto Sheriff, and Ping collides onto Pong

PRINCE *(at Sheriff)* You twit!
AUDIENCE TWOO!
SHERIFF *(at Pong)* Twit!
AUDIENCE TWOO!
PONG *(at Ping)* Twit!
AUDIENCE TWOO!

PRINCE *(getting up)* How dare you. Me, your future King.
SHERIFF Sorry, Your Highness-ship. *(brushes him down)*
PRINCE And stop calling me that.
PING *(puzzled)* He wasn't calling him 'That', he was...

He is clipped round ear by Sheriff

PRINCE I will not be surrounded by fools!

The three quickly surround him facing out, all looking about

SHERIFF Where, where are they?
PONG We'll fight them off.
PING Not a fool in sight. *(at audience)* Oh yes there is, look. *(points. Pong and Sheriff to front peering Prince John fumes goes off OPS shaking head)*
SHERIFF Oh yes, that's *(local fool)* right old fool *(he/she)* is.
PONG Look, there's another.
PING Oi, do you mind, that's my... *(mum/dad/auntie)*
SHERIFF Yes, well it does run in the family doesn't it.
PING Yes, but. Hey what do you mean by that?

As above said, Sheriff now looking around stage

SHERIFF Prince John, he's gone!
PING and **PONG** This way/That way. *(point and stick fingers in each others eyes)* Ouch/Ouch.

Sheriff looks at them then off OPS shaking head. Pong recovers first

PONG The Sheriff. He's gone! *(starts looking around)*
PING *(quivering)* Bit weird this. *(looks about front/sides)*

Pong at side. 'Shield' falls on his head, staggers round, off OPS shaking head

Can't think where they got to Pong, how about we look. *(turns)* Ooo Er. Pong. *(quivers)* Where are you Pong? *(stands centre frightened)*
PENNY *(entering PS)* It's a long journey, can I go to the... *(points, optional say, 'Er or Throne Room')*

Ping looks amazed, nods, then as going off OPS holding hands with Penny, shakes head in disbelief. Enter PS Robin and Marion arm in arm

ROBIN *(laughs)* I knew we would be together again somehow, but, for a moment there ...
MARION *(laughs)* And Fred rescued you, but I was frightened.
ROBIN Well things are more peaceful now. I just hope Lottery and Little John got there in time *(pause)* to save King Richard.
MARION At least we have a few moments together.

ROBIN Yes, *(holds hands and looks into her eyes)* my love *(pause)* listen…
MARION *(listens)* I can't hear anything. What is it?

Robin starts off and Marion joins in. Then enter PS Hera with young deer, followed by Will and Fiona, Friar (hooded cloak, but hood down) and Mystic, Dolly and Sheriff, Munch and Julie, Anna and Rob and Emma and Bob, Stinker and partner/others? All hold hands singing

SONG NO 16

THERE'S A KIND OF HUSH or LOVE IS ALL AROUND US

Music ends. Hera to Robin and Marion

HERA Did I not say be happy and enjoy your love. *(laughs)* Look at you all.

All look at each other, smile and laugh

MARION Yes Hera, and our feelings began in your magical, lovely forest.

Cistern flush, then as all looking around bemused/puzzled. Dolly squirms as if wanting to go. Enter OPS Penny looking at map, looks up and as heading off towards forest turns and waves at Ping who waves to her. All 'goodies' watch her and say, 'Ahh'. Penny off OPS, Ping sees goodies and ducks back, then as they talk as below, he pops his head out and listens

DOLLY Look everyone, Here's MY Bogey Man'
AUDIENCE IT'S NOT, HE'S NOT!
DOLLY I know we are all happy, but the Sheriff here, he's a cutie really, *(tickles under chin)* has come to join us. *(coyly clutching arm)*
MYSTIC *(exclaims)* Wondrous wonders!
SHERIFF I enjoyed the 'Be Nice Day', so much, and of course, there's the *(pause)* Hr, hm the matter of …
DOLLY My Christmas Puddings? *(squirms again)*
MYSTIC Still don't know how she makes them!
FRIAR *(blustery)* I hope you've got some left for me.
ROBIN Stop! STOP! I can't believe this. You're discussing Christmas Puddings again!
DOLLY Alright, but you must excuse me. *(squirms)* Must pay a quick visit to the, *(gestures)* you know. *(all puzzled)* THE THRONE ROOM!
MARION *(laughs)* Think I'll come too.

As ladies exit to 'Ladies', Ping disappears

SHERIFF *(laughing)* Always the same isn't it, off they go in pairs.
ROBIN We shall go and see if Lottery and Little John have returned to the Royal Oak. You two wait here for Maid Marion and Dolly. Escort them back to camp.

All exit PS as Friar and Sheriff chat and laugh

FRIAR *(serious to Sheriff)* Now listen here you. Just because Dolly likes you, I still want some of her Christmas Puddings, you're not going to get them all.

Castle doors are slammed shut. They look at each other, then rush over and bang on the doors shouting. Ping looks over parapet

PING *(sort of sings)* Yah boo, sucks to you, got the ladies locked in the loo.
SHERIFF Stop messing about, open up.
PING No fear, I'm going to tell Prince John. At least he will be pleased and not clip me round the ear!
FRIAR The Sheriff won't do it anymore, will you?
SHERIFF No, and you can visit Lucy's dungeons if you open up.
PING *(thinking)* Well, I, er, how often?
SHERIFF *(pleading)* Every day if you like...

Prince appears next to Ping - boos by all

PRINCE *(pleased)* Well done Ping. For your cleverness, YOU are now the new Sheriff of Nottingham.
SHERIFF *(exclaims)* What, that twit?
AUDIENCE TWOO!
PRINCE Yes, and he can have Lucy whip him as often as he likes.

Groans from Sheriff and Friar as they back off

PING *(beaming)* Me, Sire, the new Sheriff of Nottingham.
PRINCE Yes, you can't be any worse than that bungling fool.
PING *(smiling)* Oh I can, I can!
PRINCE Oh no you can't.
SHERIFF Oh yes he can.

OPTIONAL: Have an audience 'CAN/CAN'T' routine here as well as/instead of in Act 1, Scene 3

PRINCE We'll see. I have decided that Lady Marion shall die for her treachery, and I shall give her maid to Lucy.

'DING DONG' off

Ah, that will be Sir Guy with the good news I am expecting. *(pause)* of Richard's Death! Tomorrow, I SHALL BE CROWNED KING OF ENGLAND, and you will call me 'YOUR MAJESTY'!

Prince and Ping disappear to boos

FRIAR My goodness, what will Robin say when we tell him the Prince is going to kill Marion?

SHERIFF I don't know *(pause)* but if we don't rescue Dolly, you know what that means?

FRIAR No, what?

SHERIFF No more Christmas Puddings!

They lock aghast at each other then rush off PS as Dolly appears on parapet

DOLLY Sheriff, oh, Sheriff, oh. Wherefore art thou Sheriff, oh? *(angry)* Come back here and rescue me you, you... *(old load?)*

She is grabbed from behind by Lucy and dragged down. Castle doors opened and Ping peeps out, then enters with Pong

PING Come on Pong.

PONG What are we doing out here?

PING Sir Guy has just arrived. The Prince said to get his horse and bring it round the back.

PONG How come you're giving the orders?

PING 'Cause I'm the new Sheriff of Nottingham.

PONG What, you, you twit!

AUDIENCE TWOO!

Both exit PS and commotion off stage as they enter pulling on a high rope. During talk below, tugs on and off stage ends with Pong pulled off

PING Come here boy, *(tug)* come on now.

PONG I know Sir Guy is big, *(tug)* but I didn't know his horse was this big!

PING Probably to carry *(tug)* all that armour he wears, *(tug)* and all those weapons.

PONG Come on, nice horsey.

Optional, Ping says, "Think we need some help", then ask a few children to come up and help

PONG Stubborn old fellow isn't he?

PING Yes, bit like... *(local School Master/similar)*

PONG All together now.

PING Heave.

PONG Get him a carrot or something.

PING OK. *(lets go of rope and Pong is pulled off PS in one flying leap)*

If children, they can go/almost go, and Ping then says, 'Thank you/He'll be alright' etc., and usher back to seats, then off OPS. Enter PS, Robin, Will, Fiona, Stinker, Mystic, Munch, Julie and Merry Men/maids

ROBIN *(worried)* Still no sign of Lottery and Little John.

WILL And where have the Friar and Sheriff got to with Maid Marion and Dolly?

MUNCH Shall we go and look for them?

ROBIN Yes Munch, good idea. And keep your eye out for the King as well.

MUNCH No prob! *(scout salute/wave)*

Munch and Julie exit PS as enter PS Lottery and John

MUNCH *(acknowledging)* Hi you two, haven't seen Friar Tuck-in and the Sheriff have you?

JULIE Or Maid Marion or Dolly?

Lottery and John shake heads and go to Robin as Munch and Julie off

ROBIN Lottery, Little John, there you are, good to see you back. *(slaps on shoulders, serious)* What happened?

LOTTERY The good news or the ...

WILL *(laughs)* Bad news.

ROBIN The good news.

LOTTERY *(all gasp/shock/horror/relief as tale unfolds)*
                    I arrived to find a body all draped. *(pause)*
                    'Twas King Leopold, *(pause)* he was dead.
                    For good King Richard had escaped.
                    So Sir Guy had killed him instead.

ALL *(sort of mumble)* Good riddance/Held King to Ransom etc.,

ROBIN *(sort of OK)* Well, what's the bad news?

LOTTERY *(gestures with hand, there's more, there's more)*
                    King Richard is in England somewhere.
                    Sir Guy is trying to find him.
                    He kills all in his way without a care.
                    I fear the King's chances are slim.

General silence

MYSTIC Wo, wo, nay, a billion times wo.

WILL Well, that's a right mix of good and bad news

ROBIN Aye Will, for death is never good news.

STINKER And that Sir Guy, fearsome. I hear he cut down ten men with one blow!

ROBIN What of the ransom money, Little John?

JOHN I have taken it to the Priory for safe keeping.

Whilst below is said, all attentive to Robin, half enter PS a hooded cloaked figure (and say two similar dressed soldiers) not seen

ROBIN *(alert)* Good, but listen. we must find King Richard before Sir Guy does. Will, you and Little John take some men and search the forest and highways. Stinker, take Munch and Julie with their 'gangs' and search the villages. Do not rest until you have found our King and taken him to safety at our camp.

Hooded figures enter

KING There is no need to search, for the King is safe.
ROBIN *(turning to him)* Safe, Friar Tuck-in, but where?

Stranger(s) pulls back hood and takes robe off to reveal himself/themselves

ROBIN But you're not Friar, *(pause)* you're... Your Majesty.
All *(humbly all kneel and bow heads)* King Richard/Richard the Lionheart!
MYSTIC Wondrous wonders of wondrousness wonders!
KING Arise Sir Robin of Loxsly, *(around)* and loyal men of Sherwood.

All slowly rise

ROBIN Sire, you are indeed safe now.
KING *(serious)* Yes Robin, but I heard of *(laughs)* your roguish exploits at the tavern.
ROBIN *(laughs)* All true I hope, Your Highness.
KING *(laughs)* Aye, and I hope there is *(emphasise)* some Royal game left in my forest!
ROBIN *(sheepish)* Yes, Your Highness, *(cheeky)* though perhaps you would like to share some at our camp?
KING Yes good Robin, for there was little at the tavern.
ROBIN *(to others)* Make haste and prepare the finest meat *(laughs)* fit for a King. Will, help Munch find the ladies and Friar Tuck-in. He should be told *(laughs)* the King of England is mistaken for him, and yet yesterday, he was mistaken for a bear.

All laugh as exit PS

(to King, serious) Whilst you fought the Holy Crusades, England was troubled *(pause)* and your brother, Prince John, sent his Black Knight, Sir Guy of Gisborne to kill you.
KING What!
ROBIN Yes, Highness, even now Sir Guy seeks you out to fulfil his mission.
KING John would not have me killed?
ROBIN You underestimate him, Your Highness, for Prince John intends to be King himself! And ...

Both exit PS as Dolly rushes out OPS and round stage followed by Lucy and Ping. Stopped by Pong coming back from forest all dishevelled

PONG Trying to escape, eh?
DOLLY I'll get that Sheriff, said he'd look after me. Fly 'Over the Moon' he said.
PING Hang her! As a warning to others.

Dolly terrified. Ping points to wall and Dolly is tied by hands above head in a 'hanging' position

LUCY What now, Your New Sheriff-ship?
PING *(smiling)* Show me your whippings!

Pong clips Ping round ear as exiting OPS

Oi! That's the Sheriff's job. *(clips himself round the ear, off OPS)*

Enter PS Sheriff peering about, spots Dolly

DOLLY *(relief)* Thank goodness, 'Here's my Bogey Man'.
AUDIENCE IT'S NOT, HE'S NOT!
DOLLY *(casually)* Did you get your job back?
SHERIFF *(equally casually)* No, and what are you doing?
DOLLY *(as if obvious)* Oh, just hanging around!
SHERIFF *(laughs, deep 'Blues' accent)* Give me the Music Man.

SONG NO 17

HELLO DOLLY

Why hello Dolly, this is me Dolly,
It's nice to see you there just hanging around,
You're looking swell Dolly, I can tell Dolly,
But I know that something's gone very, very wrong.

DOLLY *(frantic)* Get me down, untie me you blithering twit!
AUDIENCE TWOO!
SHERIFF Oh, right, yes. *(grovelling)* But I came back to save you as soon as I could. The Friar and I met Robin coming back with the King, and told them about you being captured *(pause)* and Marion to be killed. Robin is gathering the men for an attack on the castle. *(frantically frees her)*

Enter OPS Prince (hears above) with Lucy, Ping, Pong and guards. As saying below, enter from audience, all crouching/creeping/darting to front, Will and Fiona in centre, Munch with Cubs and Julie with Brownies to flanks

PRINCE Ah, so my brother and Robin Hood plan to attack the castle do they. I am prepared, and with Sir Guy here, *(laughs)* he will kill Robin Hood, Lady Marion and, *(sneers)* my brother Richard. ENGLAND SHALL BE MINE!

Boos everywhere and as 'baddies' look around startled

JULIE Oh no it won't, come on... *(gang/girls/brownies)*
PRINCE *(composing)* Huh, a bunch of girls won't stop me!

Cries of, 'Yes we will' from girls

MUNCH But we will. Come on... *(gang/boys/everyone/Cubs)*

PRINCE *(composed, but agitated)* Huh, and a bunch of boys isn't going to stop me either!

Cries of, 'Yes we will' from boys

WILL With our help.

All now reach stage and start to sword fight. Fiona and Lucy (whip/dagger) Will and Pong, Munch and Ping, Julie others with soldiers. Prince now startled is backing off to castle. Enter PS Robin, John, Stinker and others

ROBIN And our help. For King and Country!

Fighting ensues as Robin has sword-fight with Prince around stage. Tasty 'Honks' and flaps. Dolly goes round gathering Puddings. Sniffer barks. Some comical bits with, 'Bash on bonce, stamp on toes, etc. Friar and King enter PS

KING Stop! STOP! There will be no more killing.

Robin hesitates, and as Prince escapes OPS

PRINCE You will never see Lady Marion again. *(off and slams doors shut)*
SHERIFF Robin, Prince John said Sir Guy will kill Lady Marion.
KING *(shocked)* But he would not kill a lady - my ward.
ROBIN No time to take chances, Maid Marion's life is at stake.

Screams off as Robin climbs up flag-pole rope and over parapet. Some fighting continues, but 'baddies' are quickly beaten. Fighting offstage as doors are opened. Robin emerges protecting Marion as fighting Prince. Fighting stops. Robin backs off as Prince appears and lowers sword

PRINCE *(gestures to inside, then to Robin)* KILL HIM!

Menacing music as first, his two metre two-handed 'broadsword' protrudes slowly, followed by Sir Guy himself. All gasp, 'Sir Guy/The Black Knight etc. Sir Guy swirls his sword around and snarls. Prince laughs

He who laughs last, laughs loudest! KILL THEM ALL!

Sir Guy moves in on Robin. Marion is terrified, and half screams as Sir Guy goes to swing sword

KILL HIM!

Enter FS Penny, followed by Fred and Twit heads down reading the map. Hera follows

PENNY *(indignant/angry)* I told you this map was wrong. *(pokes 'Golden Arrow' up Sir Guy's bottom)* Out the way you, this is a Public Footpath.

SIR GUY *(drops sword, clutches bottom)* ARRGH! *(leans backwards as turning)*

TWIT *(slightly ahead of Fred)* Hold on a minute Penny, I'm tired.

Sir Guy staggers and falls over Twit

FRED You must be tired as well Penny, let's sit down here and read this map properly.

All sit on now prostrate Sir Guy. Silence as the three slowly look up and around at astonished faces of all. Then 'goodies' cheer, 'Sir Guy beaten' etc., The three look astonished as they enjoy all the attention. The Prince has surrendered to Sheriff and Dolly. Sir Guy has now been trussed up by Cubs and Brownies, and all the weapons thrown into a pile, then quiet as Prince is taken to stand before King

KING *(sternly)* What have you to say?

PRINCE *(sort of grovel)* Richard, my brother, I thought...

KING You thought to replace me. For your treachery to me, to Lady Marion and most of all *(pause)* to my England, I banish you and your followers from these precious lands for all time. Take them away!

As being taken and Sir Guy being lifted

MUNCH A moment please, Your Majesty. *(granted)* Bob - a job.

All a little mystified as Bob gets wheelbarrow from PS and Sir Guy lifted in. As wheeled off PS

ROB He won't get away will he?

BOB No chance, we know our knots!

MUNCH Penny for Sir Guy!

All laugh/'Well done' etc.,

KING And what for you, Robin Hood?

ROBIN A pardon, Your Majesty, for all the outlaws who fought on your behalf.

KING *(looks around)* Granted, and under my rule, Saxons and Normans shall all be English free people.

ROBIN *(to all)* Long live King Richard the Lionheart!

Cheers/hurrays all round, as Dolly snuggles up to Sheriff and Tasty, and Friar to Mystic

DOLLY We're going to live with all our children. Now I've taught Tasty to lay Christmas Puddings without being frightened, we might even open a shop. And this, *(video control)* might brighten him up a bit.

FRIAR *(laughs)* Make sure *(points to Sheriff)* he's not too bright to eat all your puddings! We can buy some for our new restaurant, like... *(local popular)* Mystic has given up fortune telling, she predicted we'd make a fortune instead!

All laugh, cheer/'We'll Come' etc.,

JOHN We'll come. *(snuggles Lucy)* Lucy has given up the dark of the dungeons. We're going to live in the forest.

PING *(jumps up and down)* Goody! Can I play in the dungeons by myself now?

ROBIN What of you, Will?

WILL As Ping wasn't elected as Sheriff of Nottingham, we're going to help the new candidate - FRED!

FRED *(arms raised taking cheers)* Vote for me, less taxes.

JULIE And we're going to build a nice home for Twit...

AUDIENCE TWOO!

JULIE Not such a silly Brown Owl after all, quite wise actually!

MUNCH *(holding Penny's hand)* And, we're going to help Penny get home. *(thinks)* I have a plan. *(goes to Lottery who listens then exits)*

KING All is well then, but what of you, Robin?

ROBIN My sword and bow will always be yours, Sire, and, I... *(looks at Marion)*

KING *(laughs as looks at Marion who smiles and half nods. Takes his 'Royal Sword')* It is unlike you to be speechless Robin Hood of Sherwood. Kneel. *(Robin does so)* Your manor, lands and Earldom of Huntingdon are restored and you shall also be Baron of Sherwood and Lord of Nottingham. Arise Sir *(sword is touched on each shoulder for each title)* Earl *(starts to half laugh)* Baron, Lord Robin of Loxsly. *(Robin rises to cheers)*

MYSTIC Indeed wondrous wonders!

DOLLY With all those titles, you might one day be a LEG END.

All look puzzled

FRIAR LEG END, what on earth do you mean?

MYSTIC LEG END spelt L E G E N D. She means LEGEND, I can see it now.

All laugh as at back Lottery enters and 'kisses for luck', then throws, Bernie high off stage. Robin to Marion down on one knee. All quiet, looking at 'couple'

ROBIN *(nervous)* Milady, Marion, will, *(hesitates)* will you...

ALL Get on with it you twit!

AUDIENCE TWOO!

ROBIN Marry me?

MARION Yes, YES!

Robin rises and they hug each other. Big cheers

FRIAR *(laughs)* With all you happy couples, I'm going to be busy at the chapel.

*Music starts and 'couples' to front with Robin and Marion centre, and all sing.
Sway with clap of hands or snapping finger/thumb to tune*

SONG NO 18

GOING TO THE CHAPEL

At the end of the song, CURTAINS

SINGALONG

*After curtains have closed to prepare for the 'Noble Wedding', lights up and
Dolly, Sheriff and Fred (others?) enter. Dolly performs usual 'Singalong' start-
up banter. Start off with everyone being happy. Robin and Marion to get married,
and lots of others. Now a happy land with King Richard ruling, wonderful
being happy, etc. Only thing is, Little John and Lucy can't sleep in Sherwood
Forest very well, too many woodpeckers, have you heard them. Sheriff
demonstrate 'Ha ha ha ha ha' whilst tapping on Fred's head (or vice versa)*

SONG NO 19

IT'S THE WOODY WOODPECKER SONG

Ha ha ha ha ha, Ha ha ha ha ha,
It's the Woody woodpecker's song,
Ha ha ha ha ha, Ha ha ha ha ha,
It's the Woody woodpecker's song,

*Now children's turn (specials, birthdays etc. to stage) indicate to audience to
tap on head of person in front or to side (alternate each line OR, a mix of clap
hands/stamp feet instead) Sing and action once then split into sides to see
who can 'Ha ha ha ha ha' the loudest. Then change approach re one side first
Ha's and other side second Ha's and swap sides etc. Usual catcalls of rubbish
etc., Each side tries to outdo the other. (Dame centre doing, both sides?) As the
frivolity ends, small Chocolate Puddings, or Penguin Bars, can be given to those
on stage, then back to seats.*

ALL Well done/super/you were marvellous/we're off to the wedding now etc.
(then happy/laugh/wave as exiting)

SCENE 3b

*NOBLE WEDDING. Nottingham Castle is decorated with flags, bunting,
streamers, balloons, etc. Players enter from audience, down the centre aisle to
stage where they bow for their acknowledgements, and then move to their
assigned place ready for Robin and Marion. Suggest all costumes 'enhanced'*

for the wedding, and Fred with 'Sheriff/Mayor' outfit. Bride and Groom in
Wedding apparel. Suggested sequence order as music starts - suggest lively,
suitable wedding or similar music

Adult chorus
Juveniles in mix of costumes
Sir Guy of Gisborne and Soldiers
King Richard and Soldiers
Hera with Anna and Emma
Stinker with Rob and Bob
Sniffer, Tasty and Twit
Little John and Lucy Lockit
Will Scarlett and Fiona
Lottery and Penny
Friar Tuck-in and Mystic Mog
Ping and Pong
Fred with Munch and Julie
Sheriff of Nottingham
Dishy Dolly

After Dolly has taken acknowledgement, Lottery at side

LOTTERY   We hope you have enjoyed yourselves,
For our show is nearly over.
We end with a marriage, as all Pantos should.
Let's welcome, Maid Marion and Robin Hood.

Lottery gestures and 'wedding' music played as they enter. When on stage,
Robin and Marion to centre flanked by lead players (not blotting out little ones)
and Dishy Dolly (or Fred?) gives 'THREE CHEERS FOR ROBIN HOOD AND
MAID MARION'. Tasty comes to the fore with a box and helped by others (says,
'I said I'd get my own back') empties the contents over Robin and Marion goose
feathers. All laugh, then whole ensemble sings LEGEND

SONG 20

LEGEND

One man, one hero, one legend,
Robin Hood was born to be,
That man, that hero, that legend,
Who fought for King and country.
    Robin Hood... Robin Hood,
    A legend to love you'll agree,
    Robin Hood... Robin Hood,
    A legend of love to be free.
One man, one hero, one legend,
And merry men of Sherwood,

With sword and bow they defended,
Belief in justice and good.
   Robin Hood... Robin Hood,
   A legend to love you'll agree,
   Robin Hood... Robin Hood,
   A legend of love to be free.
One man, one hero, one legend,
His dearest was by his side,
Their love together never to end,
Maid Marion became his bride.
   Robin Hood... Robin Hood,
   A legend to love you'll agree,
   Robin Hood... Robin Hood,
   A legend of love to be free,
   A legend of love to be freeeeeee.

As final note is sung, high and loud to give a rapturous end to 'ROBIN HOOD', curtains. After the curtains have reopened for final bows and applause, Percy runs down from back of audience.

PERCY Just in time!

PENNY *(excited)* It's my brother Percy.

PERCY Thank you for your message, Munch and Lottery, we've been so worried. *(gives Bernie to Lottery)* Come on Penny, I'll take you home.

Penny hugs Percy and they hold hands. They start to walk back out, then Penny stops and turns

PENNY I'll never forget you all, thank you for helping me. Oh, I forgot, *(takes out 'Golden arrow')* this is yours, Sir, Earl, Baron, Lord Robin.

ROBIN *(laughs)* Keep it Penny, A reminder of your adventure and of how you saved my life.

ALL Good-bye Penny, good-bye everyone, GOD BLESS, GOD BLESS'

All wave as Penny and Percy skip off together

(Tradition, 'GOD BLESS' are the last words spoken in a pantomime)

FINAL CURTAINS

COSTUME NOTES

Costumes are a difficult aspect of a Pantomime. Credit should be given to those responsible for creative work and efforts backstage, before and during performances.

Costumes are as depicted in popular 'Robin Hood' books, and suitable for the whole Pantomime. All can be enhanced' for the Wedding, except perhaps Marion, Dolly and Fred. *(see below)* Costume ideas are guidelines and depend on budgets, materials and abilities; simple versions are effective. (Carousel Costumes will be pleased to assist with costume advice, or hire. Tel; 01376 572516)

GENERAL NOTE. Pantomime tradition hesitates with the colour green due to superstitions of a green carpet in tragedies, and use long ago of 'limelight'. This cast a 'greenish glow' on stage, and tended to make anything green appear invisible to the audience. However, where green is mentioned here, they are 'good roles', and with modern lighting, the superstitions need not apply.

ROBIN HOOD. Smart 'Lincoln Green' costume with hat and feather, well fitting tunic, green or brown tights etc., Gracious appearance, and soft leather belt, quiver etc., (disguise with hooded cloak/mask?)

MAID MARION. Simple, yet feminine, long flowing belted cream/soft pastel green dress, contrasting 'Royal' cape with red and gold headband/accessories. Complete period 'bridal gown for wedding, with matching tiara and bouquet.

DISHY DOLLY BROWN. Pink pyjamas are a must at times, otherwise the usual outrageous colourful 'Dame' costumes with tasteless accessories. For wedding a grand outfit with large hat.

FRIAR TUCK-IN. Monk outfit with belted waistband, and cloak.

WILL SCARLETT. Bright red hat, tunic, legging and boots.

MYSTIC MOG. Peasant style, with silvery shawl etc.,

PRINCE JOHN. Almost 'king' style with predominant gold and red colours and plenty of lace. Matching breeches and golden belt.

SHERIFF OF NOTTINGHAM. Regal smock style with loud breeches and cape/ chains as befits his position.

PING and PONG. Scruffy soldier uniforms with wide belts, big boots, tin helmets.

MUNCH. Simple beige, green and brown costume (upgrade to Scout?)

FRED. Preferably a 'golden bear', costume. Upgrade to cloak and Chain of Office for wedding.

KING RICHARD I. Royal soldier outfit, chain-mail perhaps, yet fairly simple. St. George Cross on front.

LOTTERY. Tunic top, floppy hat and matching coloured tights.

LITTLE JOHN. Tunic and tights with matching style hat.

STINKER. Smock style peasant outfit of 'Merry Men' type.

FIONA. Feminine (yellow?) warrior style outfit of the period.

JULIE. Blue and brown simple outfit enhanced to be a Guide.

HERA. Greens and browns in long flowing outfit with matching headband/train and accessories.

LUCY LOCKIT. Red or black (mix?) leather effect tight outfit, with loose chains and large bunch of keys.

SIR GUY OF GISBORNE. Black Knight outfit of chain-mail and armour, with built up shoulders.

ROB and BOB, ANNA and EMMA, Cubs and Brownies. Poor peasant costumes initially, then boys primarily as Cubs in green with gold/blue scarves accessories, and girls as Brownies in two-toned browns and gold extras.

SNIFFER. Small dog costume.

TASTY. Goose costume with some loose, pluckable feathers

PENNY and PERCY. Penguin outfits.

TWIT. Typical brown 'wise owl' costume.

MERRY MEN and MAIDS. Standard peasant style costumes.

SHERIFF SOLDIERS. Basic soldiers outfits of period.

KING'S SOLDIERS. White with red cross smock style with standard accessories.

DEER. Best kept simple with outfits/antlers/make-up.

FOREST ANIMALS. Anything suitable from existing wardrobe, or make-up.

MAKE-UP

Usual 'heavy' make-up should be used as per pantomime standards. Also, it is suggested that the faces of the juvenile characters are made to blend with the colours of their costumes.

LIGHTING, SOUNDS, SMOKE, PROPS AND STAGE NOTES

A general rule is, 'KEEP IT SIMPLE - IT WORKS'. Not so easy with Pantomimes, but we should try to stick to the principle. Much depends on the facilities of your theatre or hall, and the ideas of the Stage Manager who often has one of the hardest tasks. I am sure you will be pleased with your 'Legendary' results.

LIGHTING. Basic needs are lights, some on a dimmer switch if possible. Most aspects are self-explanatory within the text. I list below the main points which although all are not necessary, create greater excitement for the players and audience:

1. Lights or Spots (audience) Pages 6, 9, 11, 12, 14, 21, 27, 28, 31, 32, 39, 47, 54, 58.
2. Lights/Spots (stage) Pages 6, 9, 13, 15, 20, 25, 26, 28, 32, 38, 44.
3. String of coloured 'Castle' lights Page 58.
4. Flashing lights Page 9.
5 Pyrotechnics Pages 6, 9, 44.
6 Strobe lighting Page 20. (if used the normal notice **must** be posted)

SOUNDS. The sound requirements are as follows:-

1. Galloping Horses Page 18.
2. Telephone Page 25.

3. Toilet, Page 49.
4. Ding Dong, Page 50.

NOTE: If cymbals or pyrotechnics are not available, a clash on a dustbin lid should suffice. *(add other sounds as you wish)*

PROPS. The Props team are very important, making sure props are in the right place on time. It can be fun collecting them, and although something invariably goes wrong, the job should never be underestimated. This is a guideline list only, as some things depend on stage or costume aspects. I suggest that you check the list when these points have been finalised. The props are listed per scene, thus some may appear in later scenes.

ACT I, Scene 1/1a. Sign, Ale jugs, Crystal Ball, Money, Notices and pins, Wild Boar, Feathers, Arrow shafts, Video Control, Small Christmas Pudding, Mug of water, Bucket with no bottom, Carrier pigeon, Large battery with electric pads, Mutton bone./Sweets(?).
ACT 1, Scene 2/2a. Two signs, Spare staff, Silly bow and arrow, Pouch of gold, Video Control, Christmas Pudding/Large Smelling Salts with pad, Empty bucket, Squeezy bottle.
ACT 1, Scene 3. Chicken and Boar, Ale jugs, Pouch of gold, Real cooked chicken and loaf of bread, Napkin and chicken leg, Map, Glasses, Big bra, Cape or Jacket, Feathers, Pouch.
INTERVAL. *(Saturday night only)* Piece of paper with winning lottery numbers.
ACT 2, Scene 1. Two signs, Royal Shield, Two feather dusters and a broom, Crystal Ball, Several Space Hoppers/Hobby Horses/topical toys; (Optional game?) Two silly arrows, Chest of gold, Velvet cushion, Golden arrow, Slit arrow and arrow, Two puddings, Tie rope, Christmas Pudding, Large box with no bottom.
ACT 2, Scene 2. Two water filled balloons, Birthday Present, Video Control.
ACT 2, Scene 3. Three signs, Royal Shield, Very long rope, Tie rope, Two puddings, Map, Golden arrow, Tie rope, Wheelbarrow, Video Control, Carrier Pigeon.
Singalong - Noble Wedding. Chocolate Puddings/Penguin Bars, Box of goose feathers, Flags, Streamers, Bunting, Balloons, String of lights/ Carrier pigeon, Golden arrow.

Plus of course, the usual supply of signs to wave from the wings for the audience - 'BOO, BEHIND YOU, HISS, AHHH' etc.,

WEAPONS. Robin, sword, longbow, quiver, arrows, dagger. Dolly/Fred, silly bow and arrow. Friar, sword, dagger. John, staff, dagger. Sheriff, sword, dagger. Ping, Pong and soldiers, sword, dagger, crossbows, or bow and arrows. Munch, sword and dagger. King, Sword and dagger. Lottery, sword and dagger. Will/ Stinker/Merry Men, sword, bow and arrows. Fiona, sword and dagger. Lucy, whip and dagger. Julie, dagger. Sir Guy, dagger and broadsword.

STAGE. General Information. Scene descriptions are within the text and will not be covered here. No doubt you will have your own ideas, imagination, creative ability and an experienced team.

SCENE CHANGES. These should be relatively simple:-

Act 1. Sherwood Village to Forest Highway and then to Sherwood Forest. There should be ample time to complete both changes with the 'mini-routines' in front of curtains.

Act 2. Tournament to Nottingham Castle Grounds. This should not be a problem as Scene 2 is front of curtains. Also, whilst the Singalong occurs the Castle can be decorated for the 'Wedding'.

FURNITURE. The required furniture is listed below - you can of course, add or remove any as thought appropriate,

Act 1. Table and bench, Maypole, Small table and chair, Straw and Bales/ Large tree trunk, False Stream, Bush/Old table and bench, Logs, False fire and spit.

Act 2. Throne and two similar chairs. (Flags?) Two benches, Target, Pieces of Gallows/Flag with long rope.

NOTE 1. Water re stream aspect. Suggest not too much, though a 'kiddies' pool can be behind trunk, if thought appropriate. However, suggest a bowl so that Robin can make a quick splash with his hand, and perhaps a squirt from a squeezy bottle on head should give sufficient effect.

NOTE 2. Splitting the Arrow. You may have your own ideas. The following are suggested as plausible options.

1. Robin fires arrow at target. As it hits, the target is pulled over backwards by fishing line (or knocked over by onstage players) by someone offstage who was passed the line by Ping when the target was placed. The first arrow is quickly removed, and a split arrow with a Robin arrow (prepared beforehand) is put in the middle. The 'crowd' shout, 'He knocked the target over/What a shot/So powerful' etc., and pull up target for all to see.
2. A swivel target can be used, and as arrow is fired (or hidden) pyrotechnic explosion as target is swivelled over to show both arrows which were pushed in by offstage staff.
3. Julie takes out 'video control', and aims as strobe lighting, and general lights down occur. Robin 'twangs' bow but 'drops' to assistant as OPS, others rush to target with someone pulling out 'Sir Guy Arrow' and another pushes a similar to in 2 above into bulls-eye. Strobes stop and lights higher. The 'crowd' shout, 'So fast didn't see it/Faster than lightning' etc.,
4. Lottery can say slightly earlier, 'Perhaps a recharge required', and get his battery and clamps and as returning, fall over and clamp the target as Robin fires. Pyrotechnic and flash, percussion etc, and then as arrows switched by players gathering around for all to see, Friar to say 'An explosive result'.

5. Enter Penny OPS with map in hand, looks about, takes arrow from bow, wanders across the stage as pointing arrow on map, As she reaches other side, she pushes the arrow into the already split but lightly taped Sir Guy Arrow, so that it splits.

General Stage Construction. Two suggestions. The first is simple, and aimed at smaller venues, the second idea is for those performing in medium sized Village Halls or smaller theatres. *(points can be taken from both if you wish)*

1. Smaller productions. Two sets of reversible screens on casters for ease when turning. If not considered high enough, it is easy to fix an extra piece of board on top. These can be painted on directly, or have paper hung on them and painted to depict the scenes; Sherwood Village and Forest Highway on one set, and Nottingham Castle Grounds on one side of the other set, or any combination. The screens that are not in use, can be moved off, or placed behind screens being used.

Also, if other screens (angled?) are used on each side to hide behind the scenes activity, or players entry and exit, these can also be reversible with appropriate scenery. (or perhaps have a striking colour or a large painting/picture of Robin Hood.

2. Medium sized productions. Similar concepts as above, or as more room and facilities, you can expand upon them. Firstly, an assumption is made, please adapt if necessary. Available may be rear flats, side flats and two backcloths.

The side flats should be dealt with as mentioned earlier, but if not reversible, then it might be best to have a permanent theme - forest or castle on the front flats. Rear side flats need to depict three scenes - Sherwood Village, Forest Highway and Sherwood Forest. Options are open but one way to deal with this is for Sherwood Forest to be painted on the flat. The other two scenes can be painted on tabs *(cloth/canvas/stiff paper)* which have a cross strut at the top with strong twine attached. A hook is inserted at the top of flat, and by means of a pole, the tabs are hung like a picture, down to stage level. When not in use, the tabs can be rolled and stored in wings ready for the next time they are required, or hung on the back of the flat.

If possible, the back of stage flats should be used/painted with the main scene - Nottingham Castle. Then three backcloths should be painted, one with Sherwood Village, one with Forest Highway, and the last with Sherwood Forest. *(if no second backcloth is available, adopt the same principle as side Flats hang Tabs to back of stage for one of the scenes)* Alternatively, wide lengths of cloth can be tacked to top of flats, and painted accordingly. These hang down at the back when not in use, and can be 'flipped over' to stage side to show the other scene when required. Any combination of the above works well.

For more **great** pantomimes

follow

Jasper the Jester